Rather than asking how religion is transmuted into literature, we should, Denis Feeney argues, be thinking in terms of a range of cultural practices, interacting, competing, and defining each other in the process. Capitalising on recent revaluations of Roman religion by ancient historians, which have stressed the vitality and creativity of the Romans' religious system throughout its long history of continual adaptation to new challenges, this book argues that Roman literature was not an artificial or parasitic irrelevance in this context, but an important element of the dynamic religious culture, with its own status as another form of religious knowledge. Since Roman culture, both literary and religious, was so thoroughly Hellenised, the author also makes a case for a reconsideration of the traditional antitheses between Greek and Roman literature and religion, arguing against Hellenocentric prejudices and in favour of a more creative model of cultural interaction.

ROMAN LITERATURE
AND ITS CONTEXTS

Literature and religion at Rome

ROMAN LITERATURE AND ITS CONTEXTS

Series editors
Denis Feeney and Stephen Hinds

This series promotes approaches to Roman literature which are open to dialogue with current work in other areas of the classics, and in the humanities at large. The pursuit of contacts with cognate fields such as social history, anthropology, history of thought, linguistics and literary theory is in the best traditions of classical scholarship: the study of Roman literature, no less than Greek, has much to gain from engaging with these other contexts and intellectual traditions. The series offers a forum in which readers of Latin texts can sharpen their readings by placing them in broader and better-defined contexts, and in which other classicists and humanists can explore the general or particular implications of their work for readers of Latin texts. The books all constitute original and innovative research and are envisaged as suggestive essays whose aim is to stimulate debate.

Other books in the series

Catharine Edwards, *Writing Rome: textual approaches to the city*

Philip Hardie, *The epic successors of Virgil: a study in the dynamics of a tradition*

Stephen Hinds, *Allusion and intertext: dynamics of appropriation in Roman poetry*

Duncan F. Kennedy, *The arts of love: five studies in the discourse of Roman love elegy*

Charles Martindale, *Redeeming the text: Latin poetry and the hermeneutics of reception*

Literature and religion at Rome

Cultures, contexts, and beliefs

Denis Feeney

Fellow and Tutor of New College,
University of Oxford

PUBLISHED BY THE PRESS SYNDICATE OF THE UNIVERSITY OF CAMBRIDGE
The Pitt Building, Trumpington Street, Cambridge, United Kingdom

CAMBRIDGE UNIVERSITY PRESS
The Edinburgh Building, Cambridge CB2 2RU, UK   http://www.cup.cam.ac.uk
40 West 20th Street, New York, NY 10011–4211, USA   http://www.cup.org
10 Stamford Road, Oakleigh, Melbourne 3166, Australia
Ruiz de Alarcón 13, 28014 Madrid, Spain

First published 1998
Reprinted 1999

Printed in the United Kingdom at the University Press, Cambridge

Typeset in Times 9½/12 pt [VN]

A catalogue record for this book is available from the British Library

Library of Congress Cataloguing in Publication data
Feeney, Denis.
Literature and religion at Rome: cultures, contexts, and beliefs / Denis Feeney.
p.   cm. – (Roman literature and its contexts)
Includes bibliographical references and index.
ISBN 0 521 55104 8 (hardback). ISBN 0 521 55921 9 (paperback)
1. Religious poetry, Latin – History and criticism.   2. Religious drama, Latin –
History and criticism.   3. Latin literature – History and criticism   4. Mythology,
Roman, in literature.   5. Rome – Religious life and customs.   6. Religion and
literature – Rome.   7. Rome – Religion.   I. Title.   II. Series.
PA6029.R4F44   1998
870.9'382–dc21   97–6950   CIP

ISBN 0 521 55104 8 hardback
ISBN 0 521 55921 9 paperback

For my parents,
who first taught me literature and religion

Contents

Preface

I had thought it would be easier to write a short book than a long one, but I was mistaken. As I explored this large topic, I was assisted by many friends and colleagues, who generously commented on drafts, responded to questions, or made it possible for me to read their own work in draft or proof: Alessandro Barchiesi, Mary Beard, Peter Bing, Susanna Morton Braund, Jason Davies, Mary Depew, Julia Dyson, Larry Earp, Elaine Fantham, Kirk Freudenburg, Polly Hoover, Jonas Jølle, Robin Lane Fox, Jennifer Larson, Jacques Lezra, Charles Martindale, Barry Powell, Simon Price, Christopher Rowe, William Sax, Neil Whitehead, Peter Wiseman, Susanne Wofford, Tony Woodman. Among these, I owe a special debt to the careful reading and editorial acumen of Julia Dyson and Tony Woodman. I have tried out ideas, especially from the first two chapters, on many audiences: first, the Roman Society in London, and then the Universities of Chicago, Emory, Harvard, Iowa, Ohio State, Oklahoma, Pisa, Princeton, Stanford, Texas (Austin), Verona, Virginia, Washington. I trust it is not invidious to single out the following members of those audiences for special thanks: Gian Biagio Conte, Karl Galinsky, Robert Kaster, John Miller, Niall Slater, Richard Tarrant, Richard Thomas, Peter White, and Andrew Wallace-Hadrill (for his injunction 'rem tene', which I have tried always to remember). I have only myself to blame if I have not made proper use of the aid which all of the people mentioned here have given me.

My principal debt is to two friends: my co-editor, Stephen Hinds, and Terry McKiernan. To my great good fortune, from the start of my thinking about this book they have encouraged and enlightened me in many conversations and written comments on drafts; they have invari-

ably understood better than I what the argument should be. Stephen
Hinds in particular commented on successive drafts at a time when he
was himself very busy; although most pages here could have a footnote
acknowledging his insight, I must acknowledge, especially, how much I
owe to his comments on the section on hymns in the first chapter.

My editor, Pauline Hire, has been an admirably patient and encourag-
ing midwife. I owe her a particular debt of thanks for agreeing to the idea
of the series; I will always cherish the memory of the revolving bar over
Broadway in which she and Stephen Hinds and I met to plot *Roman
literature and its contexts*.

In the spirit of the series I have tried to minimise documentation; but I
have referred throughout to the most important secondary sources from
which I have learnt, so that others could learn from them as well. I have
had to cut a lot of Gordian knots; especially, I have ended up citing
Feeney (1991) more often than I would have wished, but in such a short
book economy had to triumph over modesty.

I began trying to put my thoughts on paper during a semester's leave
at the Humanities Research Institute in Madison (Spring 1993); my
warm thanks to the Senior Fellows for electing me, to my department for
releasing me, and to the other Fellows for stimulating, astringent, yet
friendly criticism of my ideas. It is a pleasure once again to thank the
Graduate School of the University of Wisconsin–Madison for summer
support in 1993, and also the Vilas Fund for summer support in 1994
and 1995.

Abbreviations of periodicals follow the system of *l'Année
Philologique*. Citations of works and collections follow the system of *The
Oxford Classical Dictionary* (2nd edn), with two exceptions: for Cicero's
letters I use the numbering system of Shackleton Bailey, and for the
fragments of Varro's *Antiquitates rerum diuinarum* I follow the numbering of Cardauns (1976). The abbreviation BNP refers to
Beard–North–Price (forthcoming), portions of which I was able to read
in typescript thanks to the great kindness of Mary Beard and Simon
Price.

Introduction

Someone writing a book on Roman literature and Roman religion would do well to begin by acknowledging that the Romans had no word corresponding to 'religion' and no word corresponding to 'literature'. Rather than being dismayed by this fact, however, we might use it to help refocus the familiar observation that in no society is there an isolated sphere, called 'Religion', set over against another, called 'Literature'. 'Literature' is not a category in nature, and nor is 'Religion' a given, which literature then addresses or reflects. Rather, when we tackle the interaction between what we call 'religion in real life' and what we call 'religion in literature', we encounter the same difficulties of referentiality and representation that have become familiar topics amongst Latinists in recent discussions of love or politics or friendship in 'real life' and in 'literature'.

In all of these areas, as G. B. Conte in particular has clearly argued, we must recognise that the 'naked facts' beloved of the empirical historicist are always 'clothed': there is no unproblematic background of reality – religious or otherwise – against which to plot the different reality of literature, since 'real life' is itself 'the locus of cultural images and models, symbolic choices, communicative and perceptual codes'.[1] In Rome there are many literary modes and there are many religious discourses, each with its own distinctive associations and semiotic features. Rather than asking how religion is transmuted into literature, then, we should instead be thinking in terms of a range of cultural

---

[1] Conte (1994), 108–10; cf. Kramer (1989), 114–15; Kennedy (1993), Ch. 1, esp. 7–8; Barchiesi (1994), esp. 'Introduzione'.

practices, interacting, competing, and defining each other in the process.

This book is written in the conviction that most Latinists are still not doing justice to the way religion and literature interact within these manifold cultural practices. The basis for that conviction, however, has shifted as I have gone along. When I began the book, I thought that the main challenge would be to argue persuasively for taking the religious aspects of the culture seriously. The process of writing it has made me realise that the main challenge is actually to find ways to counter the unspoken prejudices against taking the literary aspects of the culture seriously.

For there are many reasons why Latinists might be ill-disposed to rethink the study of Roman religion and literature. Partly, they are intimidated or unimpressed by the battery of techniques that have been evolved for the study of Greek religion and literature. Partly, they are the inheritors of a patronising attitude to Roman religion. The main reason, however, is that they are the inheritors of a patronising attitude to Roman literature. The dominant tradition of reading amongst Latinists has always been highly formalist. As a result, Latinists have tended to isolate literary texts and transform them into self-sufficient products of an autonomous and inward-turning literary tradition, cutting them off from a larger cultural context – and when that cultural context is a religious one in particular, a vicious circle makes the formalist approach appear even more natural, because tenacious conventional preconceptions about Roman religion have militated against taking that religious system seriously in the first place.[2]

Paradigms old and new

At the risk of buttressing a polarisation I am anxious to undermine, let me sketch some of the preconceptions about Roman religion that have moulded the way many critics of Roman literature have traditionally read their texts.[3] These preconceptions issued, in large part, from as-

[2] The issues and prejudices are very similar to those involved in the study of post-Classical Greek literature, for which see Hunter (1993), 1–7; Parsons (1993), 154–5.
[3] My debts to North (1986) and to Beard and Crawford (1985), 28–39, will be clear; cf. Scheid (1987); Phillips (1991a) and (1992). The traditional view is embodied in such works as Warde-Fowler (1911), but its influence continues even in such comparatively recent standard authorities as Scullard (1981).

sumptions based on either a Christian model of what counts in a religion (salvation, morality, belief) or a Greek one (ritual and mythology of corporate significance). Against these yardsticks, Roman religion was regularly viewed as oddly or quaintly formalistic, barren of emotional and ethical interest, devoid of genuine collective significance, and lacking even narratives about its divinities. Originally there may have been an admirable piety, linked to an agricultural and communal life, with simple forms of worship directed towards pleasingly primitive *numina* or aniconic deities. As time went on, however, foreign influences grew more powerful, supplying deficiencies in the system (mythology from the Greeks, personal spiritual nourishment from the Eastern mystery cults, which would eventually culminate in Christianity), but at the cost of corrupting the original nature of Roman religion into a hybrid form. The result, by the late Republic and early Empire, was a system in decline: the elite who produced and read literature, having acquired an educated scepticism from their Greek mentors, were estranged from their religious traditions, maintaining them only for the purpose of political exploitation, to fox their opponents and bamboozle the plebs. They kept their tongues in their cheeks before the old rituals of crucifying dogs and watching chickens feed, or the new hypocritical pomp of the emperor cult. The texts they read drew on a foreign mythology and did not impinge on the real world. The Hellenistic philosophical systems catered to the few who felt the need to enquire into deeper questions about human life. Genuine Roman religion survived, if at all, only in domestic or rustic piety.

This is a sketch that no one Latinist will ever have subscribed to in its entirety, but its outlines will be familiar to all. Though this model is rapidly passing out of favour, it has a powerful inertia. As far as the reading practices of many Latinists are concerned, something like this model has survived the revaluation of Roman religion that has been in full swing for the last fifteen years. Since my own working assumptions about Roman religion have been conditioned by this movement of revaluation, I should offer here a sketch, however simplified and reductive, of the emergent new model (in the full awareness that the picture is changing all the time as a result of vigorous on-going debate).

The opening salvo was fired by Jocelyn (1966), who questioned the value of judging Roman religion by the criteria of Christianity or of the Romans' Greek contemporaries, and attacked the consensus view that

Roman nobles were all religious sceptics, arguing that this view was
based upon testimonia from a tiny, and not necessarily representative,
group of self-consciously intellectual individuals (these issues of scepticism and belief will claim our attention in Chapter 1). He demonstrated
how integral the religious system was to the functioning of the state and,
especially, how important it was to the Roman nobles, who might be
priests and augurs as well as governors and generals. According to
Jocelyn, Roman politicians 'must have felt that the traditional rites and
ceremonies were not immutable duties owed to the powers of another
world but rather means of utilizing certain kinds of power in their own
world. This was a state of mind not easily shaken by rationalist criticism.'[4] Subsequent studies have continued to stress the interpenetration
in the *res publica* of the 'political' and the 'religious' (categories precipi-
tated out as separate terms only by modern Western thought), emphasis-
ing that it was the elite themselves who paid for and oversaw organised
religious activity and who were most affected by its operation.[5] These
eminently practical and busy people devoted enormous amounts of time
and money to their religious practices, constantly innovating and reforming, in elaborate and complex ways. Far from being desiccated and
pointless, the various forms of public religious activity were among the
elite culture's principal venues for individual self-advertisement and
corporate self-definition.

Simultaneously, the concept of 'decline' has been called into question
by scholars who have argued for the flexibility and responsiveness of the
system in the face of the transformations which Roman society under-
went in the evolution from Latin city-state to world empire.[6] The Romans' obsessive talk of conservation and tradition has obscured the
imaginative power with which they responded to their centuries-long
series of encounters with the new and strange (as often, a parallel with
the Japanese suggests itself). Religious adaptation is a part of this
process, and was so from the very beginning, so that the search for an
original, 'natural' Roman religion, pure of foreign influence, has come to

---

[4] Jocelyn (1966), 101.

[5] Weinstock (1971); Liebeschuetz (1979), 15–20; MacMullen (1981), 24–5, 129; Price
(1984), 15–16; Scheid (1985), 12–13; Phillips (1986), 2708–9; Beard (1994), 729–34.
On the inapplicability of our categories of 'political/religious' to, e.g., Islam, see
Asad (1993), esp. 28–9.

[6] North (1976); Wardman (1982); Beard (1994), 739–45.

look more and more fantastic: in religion, as in other spheres, one must acknowledge the power of T. J. Cornell's observation that 'an independent or autonomous Latin culture never had a chance to emerge'.[7] Interaction with foreign religious systems, although varying in degree and nature at different times, is an integral part of Roman religion, not necessarily a symptom of decline or inadequacy.

Similarly, the evidence concerning the late Republic which had conventionally been used to argue for a religious malaise has been reinterpreted in different ways. The emphasis on religious decline may be seen as an element of the crisis-atmosphere needed by the new principate to legitimise its continuance.[8] Further, the very profusion of speculation is a sign of an explosion of knowledge and interest, which entailed its own paradoxical dangers: the process of supersession and decay, for example, natural in a longstanding polytheistic system, may appear alarming and novel once it begins to be documented by a new intellectual tradition.[9] As a result of increased specialisation in Roman life, it was now possible to begin to define 'religion' as an object of enquiry for the first time; if critical or sceptical forms of enquiry were inevitably one consequence, we should not be misled into overlooking the intellectual and social creative energy which made such investigation possible in the first place.[10] Besides, what we might regard as new-fangled scepticism is arguably one manifestation of long-enduring attitudes within the Romans' turbulent political life, where the meaning of divine signs had always been debated: 'it is likely that sophisticated scepticism with regard to purported divine signs was an integral part of Roman *mos maiorum*'.[11]

The revisionists' emphasis on the importance of public cult was necessary as a reaction against earlier disparaging attitudes, ultimately grounded in Christian assumptions, which had often neglected public cult in a misguided search for a supposedly more genuine and meaningful religious experience in some private or domestic sphere. Recently, however, there are signs of a newly dynamic interest in the interactions

---

[7] Cornell (1978), 110; cf. Tomlin (1974), 156, on Japan: 'there has never been an authentic Japan which was not also a Japan avid to assimilate outside influence. That *is* the authentic Japan' (original emphasis).   [8] Edwards (1996), 49–50.

[9] North (1976); Wardman (1982), 8.

[10] Beard (1986) and (1994), 755–61; North (1986).   [11] Liebeschuetz (1995), 315.

between 'public' and 'private' religion.[12] Just as recent studies of Roman
social life have been revealing the 'interpenetration of the public and
private life of the Roman ruling class',[13] so the boundary between private
and state religion is looking increasingly permeable. Public and private
cults could track each other in various ways,[14] and the gods worshipped
in the house were not divorced from the gods of public cult. The cult of
the Penates involved domesticated deities from public cult (Jupiter and
Minerva, Fortuna, Hercules), who were worshipped by the free members
of the household;[15] the Lares Familiares were worshipped by everyone in
the household, including slaves. The picture is one of a continuum of
linked chains: from the master's point of view, the Lares are primarily a
focus for mediation and self-representation 'down' or 'within', while the
Penates are a focus 'up' or 'outside'. As further confirmation of the '(to
us) astonishingly public nature of domestic life', the main venues for
display of domestic cult objects were places where guests would be
expected, in the more 'public', not 'private' parts of the house.[16] The
house, and the house's religion, are not a private retreat for such people,
for the religious categories of public and private are as porous as the
social. Clearly, then, a new debate on what counts as private or public in
Roman piety is beginning, one which looks set to transcend the earlier
altercations over whether quintessential Roman religion was fundamentally public or fundamentally private.

The Greek model

If we try to fit the category of 'literature' into these discussions, we find
ourselves, not for the last time, up against the problem of the Greek
model. Of course, discussion of Roman culture in general has been
handicapped by invidious comparisons with the Greek counterpart ever
since the Romantic movement, when Rome became 'not-Greece', a
system of lack.[17] But when we come to judge the question of the religious
element in literature, the Roman pan of the scales falls remorselessly, for
long-engrained reading practices automatically attribute cultural power

---

[12] North (1989), 604–7 and (1995).   [13] Wallace-Hadrill (1994), 60.
[14] North (1989), 606.   [15] Bakker (1994), 40–3.
[16] Wallace-Hadrill (1994), 60; Bakker (1994), 179–80 for placement of cult objects.
[17] Habinek (1992); on religion and mythology in particular, see Phillips (1991a) and
(1992), esp. 60–3; Beard (1993).

to Greek literature in its religious dimension, and just as automatically deny it to Roman. In Greece, after all, or at least in pre-Hellenistic Greece (for periodisation is significant here), the *communis opinio* has it that there was an authentic, lived religion, in which an authentic art had its roots, nourishing and nourished by a rich religious discourse shared by the society as a whole. It does not matter how that religious discourse is redefined by the changing paradigms of modern scholarship; the result is always an organic way of reading Greek literature. Thirty years ago, for example, we used to be told that the Athenians gathered together once or twice a year at the tragic festivals to learn profound truths about theology; now, after the structuralist revolution, we know that they gathered together to learn profound truths about sociology. Whatever its other claims, structuralism has proved to be yet another way of furthering a project dear to European culture since Romanticism, that of maintaining a holistic interpretation of the Greek experience. Its great success in this is not to be wondered at, since its *modus operandi* is to show that everything in the system relates somehow to everything else, which is what Romantics have always wanted to believe about the Greeks anyway.

In Rome, on the other hand, the prevalent assumption has been, as we have seen, that there was no authentic religious experience in the first place. The contrast with scholarly attitudes to Greece in this respect can be revealed even in such tiny matters as the tense used for describing the practices of the different religions: the norm for scholars of Greek religion is the anthropological present, whereas the proper tense for descriptions of Roman religion is the antiquarian imperfect. If there was such a thing as an authentic Roman religious experience, according to the usual view, it was a humble piety that had either vanished before Roman literature began, or else, if it survived in any form, had no ties of any power with the Grecising formalist literature of the elite. The kind of natural symbiosis that scholars instinctively search for in the Greek world appears not to be part of the Roman experience, and the literature that touches upon religious concerns or myth must therefore be marked down as artificial, part of a fantasy-world, or even – harshest condemnation of all from a classicist – a 'literary exercise'. The traditional disregard for the cultural power of Roman religion joins in a powerful conspiracy with the long-engrained aestheticising tendency in the study of Roman literature. In this regard, at least, the revolution in the study

of Roman religion has left most Latinists' reading habits practically
unscathed, despite some dramatic examples of attempting to cut the
Gordian knot.[18]

The problems posed by this Greek/Roman antithesis will engage us
throughout the book. The antithesis is not one we can avoid, for the
assumptions of modern criticism and religious studies are so firmly
grounded in it: the Greek/Roman antithesis remains our foremost
example of the myth of imitative impotence, of an original which is then
weakened. Whatever we say about the Roman experience in this department will be in dialogue with the Greek experience, and the dialogue
might as well be voiced rather than mute. Nor, of course, was the
antithesis one that the Romans themselves could avoid, since their own
culture – however self-consciously Roman – was so radically Hellenised,
most obviously in their literature, which they remembered as beginning
when a Greek man translated a Greek dramatic script into Latin. One of
the principal aims of this book is to suggest that we recast the antithesis
in ways which do not inevitably project the Romans as 'secondary',
passive and inert, but rather as participants in a dynamic and revolutionary cultural process. In this way, we may be able to see how Hellenism
discharged for the Romans a function analogous to that which Jonathan
Z. Smith describes Judaism discharging for the modern Christian student of religion, since it is:

> close, yet distant; similar, yet strange; 'occidental,' yet 'oriental';
> commonplace, yet exotic. This tension between the familiar and the
> unfamiliar, at the very heart of the imagining of Judaism, has enor-
> mous cognitive power. It invites, it requires comparison. Judaism is
> foreign enough for comparison and interpretation to be necessary; it
> is close enough for comparison and interpretation to be possible.[19]

---

[18] Esp. Beard (1993).
[19] Smith (1982), xii. From this perspective my book is another chapter in the ceaseless
debate about the Greek and the Roman in Latin literature, and behind the discussion lie such masterpieces as Fraenkel (1960), Williams (1968), and Griffin
(1985). Every generation of Latinists has to reinvent this wheel, just as every
generation of Romans did: see Ch. 3 ('Diachrony: Literary history and its narratives') of Hinds (1998).

Agenda

The issue of the Greek paradigm, although important throughout, will be most pressing in the first two chapters, 'Belief' and 'Myth'. The topic of belief is much larger than the issue of elite scepticism, which has traditionally engrossed so much attention. In examining what it means to speak of belief in an ancient religious context, we will need to pare away many layers of assumptions, beginning with the idea that belief is a constant feature of religious activity, or that an ancient society offered in the first place a unitary 'something', a 'religion', which is there to be 'believed in' and used as a homogeneous background for literature to work against. Following in the path of Paul Veyne, I shall document the variety of religious discourses in Rome and Greece, and then discuss the problem of how the diverse religious discourses interact both with each other and with the various literary discourses. Although it may appear that the co-existence of these different genres of belief is testimony to a lack of energy or significance in any one of them, I shall argue that the competitive interaction between the genres of belief is instead fruitful and dynamic, being productive of meaning. Roman literature is not parasitic or self-deprecatory in this regard, but self-conscious about the way in which it has functions and capacities not available to the other discourses. A major test case will be provided by the relationship between Augustus' *ludi saeculares* and Horace's *carmen saeculare*, whose performance was the culmination of three days of ritual.

When we come to 'Myth', deep excavation is also necessary in order to unearth the factors that have traditionally handicapped the study of myth in Roman culture. Most important of these are the usually unarticulated prejudices that have their origin in a Hellenocentric view of mythopoesis. The Romantic view of an organic and natural Greek mythic process has become naturalised in the culture at large and amongst professional scholars. The allure of the oral and the primary has smothered the study of myth in the aggressively literate and adaptive society of Rome. Here it will be necessary to question the value of this Hellenocentric model of myth, not only in its misapplication to the world of the Romans, but also in its own Greek context.

After belief and myth, we will turn to 'Divinity', a topic which even today many might regard as not particularly urgent in a Roman setting. A now outmoded view denied so much as anthropomorphism to the earliest Roman divinities, speaking rather of *numina* or – yet more awesome – *mana*. Jocelyn's functionalist methodology, intent on elucidating the social dimension of Roman religion, rather depreciates the importance of the gods as entities to be encountered or negotiated with: 'the traditional rites and ceremonies were not immutable duties owed to the powers of another world but rather means of utilizing certain kinds of power in their own world' (above, p. 4). Yet an appreciation of how the Romans figured the gods as participants or persons, so far from being irreconcilable with a functionalist approach, might help to shed light on how they represented power and structure in the city and empire. This is a difficult undertaking, however, for the question of the gods' personalities remains problematic in many ways. They had their images, their houses (*aedes*), their couches, and their public parades; they were the addressees of prayer and the recipients of sacrifice; their nature, categories, and powers were much discussed. All these challenging forms of representation are put to the test in a wide range of literary and non-literary contexts. For a society that was well accustomed to manipulating such forms of representation, the nature of divinity takes on an acutely pressing importance when the most important men in the state begin probing at its limits, becoming objects of cult and inhabitants of temples themselves.

With 'Ritual', we would seem to be on firm Roman footing, for the revaluation of Roman religion has put the spotlight on public cult in ways which would have astonished a Latinist of the last generation. Dismissed for so long as sterile and frigid, an empty formality, a poor substitute for the corporate self-expression of the festivals of the *polis*, Roman civic cult has become a trump card: if you can prove that something has a reference to cult, you are proving it means something. Hence, in part, the striking rehabilitation of Ovid's *Fasti*, a poem which even ten years ago was in effect out of the canon. But ritual is not a self-explanatory system, and it remains a challenge to analyse how Roman writers make the meaning systems of ritual part of the meaning systems of their texts.

The revaluation of ritual in a Roman context is to some degree a result of the feeling that this is one area at least in which the techniques and successes of structuralism can be transplanted from the Greek field. In fact, however, this new focus on ritual ends up perpetuating a long-standing assumption that the automatic place to seek for the 'essentially

Roman' element of religion is in cult. While attempting to do justice to the modern and ancient fascination with ritual, with Ovid's *Fasti* as the main focus, this chapter will argue that the effort to define ritual as the authentically Roman element in literature or in religion is liable to be a misguided exercise in nostalgia – although one which the Romans themselves were already cultivating.

Lastly (not firstly), 'Knowledge'. The Romans' religious system was vast and ramshackle, with no revealed text at its core and no overseeing body. The simple issue of how Roman writers got information about religion is interesting in itself, but since Foucault it has not been possible to think of knowledge as just a matter of information. What kind of knowledge-systems were there? How did they interact with and define one another? Whose interests did they serve? By the early principate there were mountains of written material on every conceivable topic, practically all of it now lost. You could read books on augury, extispicy, astrology, on thunder-interpretation, priesthoods, and deities native and foreign. Some of the priestly colleges had their own written texts. A consideration of how all these diverse forms of material relate to one another, and to the texts we call 'literary', will lead us back to the problems of the interactions between genres of belief with which the book begins.

CHAPTER

I

Belief

Twenty or thirty years ago it would have been relatively uncontroversial to state that educated Romans of historical times did not seriously believe in their gods or in state rituals or in emperor cult; that any core of real belief must have been located in domestic rites, not public ones; that no one believed in the foreign myths imported from Greece. All such statements have since become problematic, not so much because people now claim that the Romans did in fact believe in all these things and in all these ways, but because the meaning and relevance of the term 'belief' have been called into question.

The anthropologists have not omitted belief from their enquiries into the perils of transferring culturally bound categories from one society to another. Belief was the subject of perhaps the most famous such enquiry, that of Needham, who argued that there was no ground for 'the received idea that this verbal concept corresponds to a distinct and natural capacity that is shared by all human beings'.[1] 'Belief', according to this view, is a concept entirely specific to European Christian culture, the consequence of the great importance given in Christian religion to 'belief' in the central doctrines of resurrection and redemption. Warnings against 'Christianising' interpretations of Roman religion have therefore become topical in modern studies.[2] It is, indeed, arguable that

---

[1] Needham (1972), 191. Needham is much indebted to Wittgenstein's approach to the radically contextual nature of meanings of the word 'belief', on which see Malcolm (1994), 44–7.

[2] Price (1984), 10–15; Beard and Crawford (1985), 26–7; Phillips (1986), 2697–711 (with valuable reservations on the language of 'belief'). The danger in this antithetical construction of a monolithic 'Christianity' is that it papers over the fissures separating the High Anglican from the Southern Baptist; see further below, p. 15.

the very concept of 'religion' as an entity to be found in all cultures is itself the work of Christian presuppositions.[3]

However that may be, when tackling the problem of what we call 'belief' in what we call 'Roman religion', we should – to put it most modestly – bear in mind that not all religions place as high a value on belief in key dogmas as does modern Christianity. The Japanese again suggest themselves as a parallel for the Romans; the very word for 'religion' in Japanese was coined only in the nineteenth century after contact with the West, 'to denote a concept and view of religion commonplace in the realms of nineteenth-century Christian theology but at that time not found in Japan, of religion as a specific, belief-framed entity'.[4] According to Pettazzoni, the Shintoism of Japan belongs not with the 'modern' religions of Christianity, Buddhism, and Islam, which are characterised 'by the presence of a founder, by a soteriological ideal, by proselytism, by supernationalism', but with the 'ancient' religions of the Romans, Greeks, Hittites, and Aztecs, which remember no founder, seek no converts, and aim not at the salvation of the individual in a future life but at the preservation and growth of the community in this one.[5]

This is not to say that language of belief is never an issue when we are discussing the 'ancient' religions. It certainly is, as we shall see in detail. The point, however, is that it is not legitimate to proceed on the assumption that there is a discrete core of belief lurking somewhere at the heart of any religious system, or to measure the worth of ancient religious experience against a yardstick of how emotionally meaningful or belief-laden it was.[6] A dynamically changing polytheistic system is an exceedingly problematic place in which to find the grounding for a question like

[3] So Balagangadhara (1994): 'the reason for believing that India knows of religion is religious in nature' (149; cf. 260–1); cf. Asad (1993), esp. 40–3, 54, and Staal (1989), 393, on the Western *creation* of so-called religions' (original emphasis). Balagangadhara (1994) makes thought-provoking comparisons between Indian and Roman conditions: 33–46, 486–90.

[4] Reader (1991), 13; cf. Staal (1989), 335, 389–90, on the absence of belief or doctrine and the importance of ritual practice in Hinduism and Buddhism. On the Japanese as a parallel for the Romans, above, p. 4.

[5] Pettazzoni (1972), 28–9; cf. Goodman (1994), on the different attitudes to membership and proselytising shown by pagans, Christians, and Jews.

[6] Price (1984), 10–11; cf. R. Needham's introduction to Hocart (1987), 5–6, for a critique of explanations of social institutions that are grounded in individual psychology.

'What were the religious beliefs of Augustus?'. This man – as we at least describe him – was participant in and object of various new and traditional cults at Rome and throughout the Empire, and an initiate into the mysteries of Eleusis since the age of thirty-two. He was acclaimed in marble, bronze, papyrus and song as the descendant of Venus and the son of Divus Julius. He was the vice-regent of Jupiter, founder of a new temple of Jupiter the Thunderer, and always carried a sealskin with him as protection against thunderstorms. In which of these contexts is the 'core' of belief to be found?

Addressing the problem of belief is not simply a matter of tallying up all the evidence for scepticism in one column and all the evidence for credulity or allegiance to cult in another. For any given period, and for many given individuals, there will be numerous items in both columns. This anecdotal procedure, however, would not help us, partly because it is still locked in to Christian presuppositions (there is a core to which one accords, or from which one withholds, belief), but mainly because it does not provide a context for assessing these discrete items of information.

Brain-balkanisation

Much the most helpful starting-point is provided by Paul Veyne's *Les Grecs ont-ils cru à leurs mythes?*, with its 'plurality of modalities of beliefs', a notion which even in 1983 he could describe as 'too much of a commonplace for it to be necessary for us to dwell on it'.[7] Drawing in an eclectic and undoctrinaire manner on the anthropological insights of Sperber (1975) and on the discourse-theory of Foucault, Veyne did not rest with the idea that truth-criteria are historically contingent, but went on to recreate a world which lived with various programmes of truth and 'modalities of belief'. His marvellous phrase 'balkanisation des cerveaux' ('brain-balkanisation') captures the capacity of educated Greeks and Romans of the post-classical era to entertain different kinds of assent and criteria of judgement in different contexts, in ways that strike the modern observer as mutually contradictory. These people are involved in very different activities when they sacrifice outside a temple, talk to the custodian of a temple, read the aretalogy inscribed outside the

---

[7] English translation (1988), 135 n. 33; cf. 87, 'truth is plural and analogical'. See now Buxton (1994), 155–64.

temple, read the scholar Apollodorus' book *On the Gods*, listen to hymns, read Homer allegorised or Homer rationalised, read an epic on Heracles, or read about Heracles the supreme commander in a history. Expressions of scepticism are always potentially part of the procedure, for the participants' assent may be provisional, self-consciously in tension with dissent.

In the spirit of Veyne's eclecticism we might refer here to a range of related approaches, all of which stress the contingent and contextual nature of belief-systems, and all of which concentrate on the dissonance that presents a stumbling block to monolithic interpretations: the work of Versnel (1990) and (1993) on 'Inconsistencies in Greek and Roman religion', informed by psychological studies of 'cognitive dissonance'; the work of anthropologists such as Sperber on the vital importance of contextualising inconsistent and unstable belief systems;[8] the work on social roles by sociologists such as Gouldner, according to whom 'it is of the essence of social roles that they never demand total involvement by the actors, but only segmental and partial involvement';[9] Foucault's discourse-theory, which sees truth within a society not as a universal entity but as something constituted severally by particular truth-producing systems.[10] None of these approaches takes its final object of enquiry to be the private mental world of a participant, for that world is ultimately inaccessible, and the individual's psychology cannot be the ground for social institutions. Rather, the object of enquiry is the particular system of rules appropriate to any given context of speech or action, together with the wider practice which regulates that system of rules. Even modern Christian society, whose supposedly monolithic belief system Veyne tends to hold up as diametrically opposed to the splintered world of the ancient intellectual, is analysable along the same lines – witness the splendid parodic title of an article on Veyne by a French anthropologist, Méheust (1990), 'Les Occidentaux du XXᵉ siècle ont-ils cru à leurs mythes?'.

The ancients had their own way of framing this kind of issue, with their doctrine of the 'three theologies', three ways of talking about the gods. This influential model, the product of long-standing debates and prejudices, was developed in the Hellenistic period and applied to Rome

[8] Sperber (1985), esp. 48; cf. Bell (1992), esp. 182–7.   [9] Gouldner (1973), 210.
[10] E.g. Foucault (1978), 92–102, esp. 100–1.

by Varro in the 40s BCE. The three theologies – of the poets, the state, and the philosophers – were each said to have a quite distinct nature, origin, and function.[11] The first line of Lucretius' *De rerum natura* presents all three in sequence: *Aeneadum genetrix, hominum diuumque uoluptas* ('Mother of the Aeneadae, of men and gods the pleasure'). The goddess' political persona comes first, as a patron-goddess of the Roman state and of the family of Lucretius' addressee, Memmius; next is a pair of genitives from the register of Ennian and Homeric epic, capped by the key word of Epicurean ethics, 'pleasure' (ἡδονή).[12] The three dominant ways of apprehending a religious phenomenon are put in play from the moment the poem begins.

The degree of 'brain-balkanisation' of the educated Roman can be very difficult to appreciate. We are dealing with more than literary or social decorum, of the kind that Latinists recognise operating when, for example, Cicero talks of the gods' direct guidance and support against Catiline in a speech to the people but not in a speech to the Senate, or disparages his own earlier epic account of divination while conducting philosophical investigation into the topic, or apologises for his lengthy mythological excursus on the rape of Proserpina and the cult of Ceres during a speech prosecuting a Roman magistrate; or when (a harder case) the same Seneca who composed mythological poetic dramas denounces the trivial untruths of the poets in his philosophical treatises.[13]

Even within one category, such as the philosophical discussion of religion, we find strongly demarcated sub-divisions. Momigliano, for example, expresses surprise that Cicero's philosophical dialogues completely bypassed the mounds of antiquarian material about Roman religion amassed by Varro in his *Antiquitates rerum diuinarum*. The explanation, he concludes, is that it was just impossible for a sensible man to 'believe in all these divine forces' on parade in Varro's work (Adeona, Abeona, Interduca, Domiduca . . .)[14] Yet the conversation staged by Cicero between himself and Varro at the beginning of the *Academica* self-consciously reflects upon the fundamental distinction

---

[11] Lieberg (1973); for Augustine *De civ. D.* 6.5, our major source for Varro's system, see BNP, vol. 2 no. 13.9.   [12] Kenney (1977), 11.

[13] Mack (1937), 76, Goar (1972), 40–5 and Vasaly (1993), 86–7 on the *Catilinarians*; Schofield (1986), 58, Timpanaro (1988), lxxvii-lxxx and Feeney (1991), 260 on *Div.* 2.45–7; *Verr.* 2.4.109 on Proserpina and Ceres; Hutchinson (1993), 17–18, 187, on Seneca.   [14] Momigliano (1987), 64–5.

between Cicero's kind of composition and Varro's. Cicero is writing high philosophy, in a tradition that goes back to Plato, but the antiquarian Varro wants nothing to do with this form of endeavour, and goes so far as to claim that educated Romans can go directly to the Greeks for Greek philosophy (*Acad. Post.* 1.3–4). Varro (Cicero's character, that is) claims that only in the introductory sections of his *Antiquitates* was he writing for philosophers (*in his ipsis antiquitatum prooemiis philosophis scribere uoluimus*, 8). Cicero's presentation here seems to reflect Varro's procedure quite accurately, for Varro devoted only the first book of the *Antiquitates rerum diuinarum* to expounding the three theologies and various doctrines of mind and body, before presenting his collected material on priesthoods, festivals, and cult in the remaining fifteen books.[15]

The era's two most systematic and intelligent commentators on 'religion', then, are coming at the topic from two quite different angles, and it would be a great mistake to come to any conclusions concerning what Cicero or Varro or their contemporaries 'really believed' about Roman religion on the basis of these self-conscious demarcations between generic and intellectual traditions. Further, Cicero himself can adopt quite different poses in different philosophical dialogues, with different consequences for his apparent opinions on such important matters as divination: 'in the *De re publica* and *De legibus* Cicero discourses and legislates as a *princeps civitatis*; in the *De natura deorum* and *De divinatione* he presents his views as a philosopher'.[16]

Profound discursive distinctions are to be found outside philosophers' books as well. Fissures that would startle practically any modern observer appear, for example, in the evidence for the cult of the Dea Dia, the goddess who was served by the Fratres Arvales. This is easily the best documented cult we have, with yards of inscriptions surviving from her grove outside the city, containing detailed descriptions of dozens of cult acts, and including the names of some 180 priests.[17] It is clear that many educated and well connected people put a great deal of energy into this activity. Yet literary sources leave us almost completely in the dark concerning the cult. If the cult site had not been found we would know that there was a priesthood of Fratres Arvales, and we would have some

---

[15] Rawson (1985), 313–14.   [16] Linderski (1982), 22–3.
[17] BNP, vol. 2 nos. 4.5 and 6.2.

stories giving an aetiology for the priesthood, but we would not know so much as the name of the goddess they honoured or the place where they honoured her.[18] Conversely, the documentation of the cult site has not a word to say about the topics discussed by the literary sources (the aetiological story of Romulus and Acca Larentia, for instance).[19]

The cult of Bona Dea presents a perhaps even more perplexing case. Although here we have much more literary discussion of the cult to supplement the extensive epigraphic evidence, nonetheless, as the author of a recent exhaustive study of Bona Dea says, 'the two kinds of sources – archaeological-epigraphic and literary – barely complement each other to produce a uniform picture. They rather seem to contradict each other in a not inconsiderable number of instances.'[20] In particular, the literary sources show us a cult which is aristocratic, part of the state religion, observed exclusively by women of the elite, and confined to the city of Rome: the epigraphic evidence shows us males, foreigners, slaves and freedmen amongst the worshippers, and a host of personal and private dedications throughout Italy and (sporadically) the whole Empire.[21] These two pictures have practically nothing in common apart from the name of the goddess. Another example of such a phenomenon is to be found in the cult of Silvanus, where the discrepancies between the literary and epigraphic evidence are similar, although rather less dramatic.[22]

If there are disparities between the pictures presented of a single deity's cult by literary and non-literary sources, we may observe further that even the same divine name may cover many different cults in the city. Venus Erycina on the Capitol was connected with Mens ('Mind', 'Right Thinking'), but Venus of the Porta Collina was especially honoured by prostitutes – and elsewhere in the city you could find Venus Calva, Felix, Genetrix, Hortorum Sallustianorum, Libitina, Obsequens, Verticordia, Victrix.[23] Here we are presented with yet another kind of challenge to deciding what is meant by 'believing in' a god.

By this kind of analysis, then, what we label 'Roman religion' is not a single item for investigation, let alone a thing to be believed in or not. Nor is the defining mental attitude of the hypothetical believer a recoverable object of study, something which remains a constant over the range

[18] Scheid (1990), 39.   [19] Scheid (1993), 112.   [20] Brouwer (1989), XXVI.
[21] Brouwer (1989), 257–9, 297–301.   [22] Dorcey (1992), 1.
[23] Dumézil (1970), 492 on the Capitol and Porta Collina.

of contexts we have been glancing at here. Rather, many modes of belief criss-cross the entire field, interpenetrating in the same person and in the same literary work.[24] Cicero is a particularly fine example – a producer of a tremendous range of writing (including even epic poetry) in which religion figured very diversely; possessed of a 'religiously cold temperament', according to Veyne, and someone who speaks to his wife as if the cult of the gods were more her responsibility than his;[25] yet ostentatious in his cultivation of Minerva in times of personal political crisis, and, most strikingly, obsessed for months with the private project of a *fanum*, 'shrine', for his dead daughter, one which should achieve 'apotheosis' for her.[26]

Even Julius Caesar, so often held up as the archetypal Roman rationalist and sceptic, presents a more fractured picture upon closer inspection. First of all, his austerely rationalist *Commentarii*, devoid of reference to the Roman military-political apparatus of auspices and omens, are interestingly at odds with the mass of other evidence for his obsession with all kinds of cult, including his own.[27] Yet the *Commentarii* themselves are not as straightforward in this regard as they are usually painted. The absence of auspices and omens from the *Commentarii* is regularly attributed to the educated scepticism of author and upper-class audience alike;[28] but this conclusion is disturbed by Caesar's single citation of a mass of omens, artfully postponed until after his arrival in Asia following the crowning mercy of Pharsalus (*B. Civ.* 3.105.3–6):

Item constabat Elide in templo Mineruae repetitis atque enumeratis diebus, quo die proelium secundum Caesar fecisset, simulacrum Victoriae quod ante ipsam Mineruam collocatum esset et ante ad simulacrum Mineruae spectauisset ad ualuas se templi limenque conuertisse. eodemque die Antiochiae in Syria bis tantus exercitus clamor et signorum sonus exauditus est ut in muris armata ciuitas discurreret. hoc idem Ptolomaide accidit. Pergamique in occultis ac reconditis templis, quo praeter sacerdotes adire fas non est, quae Graeci adyta appellant, tympana sonuerunt. item Trallibus in templo Victoriae,

[24] Cf. Levene (1993), 241, on Livy: 'Religion in Livy is not a single monolithic entity.'
[25] Veyne (1988), 49; Cic. *Fam.* 6.1, 155.1.
[26] Courtney (1993), 158 for the evidence concerning Minerva. Cic. *Att.* 254 is the first of a long series of letters to Atticus about the *fanum*; 259.1 and 275.1 on ἀποθέωσις. [27] Weinstock (1971). [28] Linderski (1982), 36.

ubi Caesaris statuam consecrauerant, palma per eos dies . . . inter
coagmenta lapidum ex pauimento exstitisse ostendebatur.

Likewise it was established by counting back the total number of days
that in the temple of Minerva at Elis, on the day that Caesar had
fought his successful battle, a statue of Victory which had been placed
in front of Minerva and had formerly faced the statue of Minerva had
turned around towards the doors and threshold of the temple. On the
same day, at Antioch in Syria, on two occasions there had been heard
such a loud noise of an army shouting and trumpets sounding that the
people put on armour and rushed to defend the walls. This same thing
happened at Ptolemais. And in Pergama, in the hidden and secret
temples, where it is forbidden for anyone but the priests to enter (the
Greeks call them *adyta*), drums sounded. In Tralles, likewise, in the
temple of Victory, where they had dedicated a statue of Caesar, they
pointed out a palm tree which had sprung up in that period out of the
pavement between the joints of the stones.

This irruption into the measured prose of senatorial despatches comes
with the effect of a thunderclap after ten volumes' silence on divine signs.
We could say that Caesar systematically suppressed the familiar details
of Roman military-political divination because he did not really believe
in it, and that the Asian omens amount to a definitive and culminating
revelation of what he did really believe. It is more fruitful, however, to
see that both strategies, in their different ways, highlight the great
individual's emancipation from the traditional apparatus. What we see
as 'rationalism' is a way of showing the *imperator* to be independent of
the conventional religious and political guarantees of success, and the
Asian omens of victory serve a similar function: the traditional state
apparatus of the *res publica* is being superseded by the manifestation of
divine favour for the spectacular charismatic individual.[29]

To supplement this anthropological or sociological perspective, we
need also to remind ourselves of the related problems of literary reference discussed at the beginning of the Introduction. If 'belief' is a

[29] On this development in the late Republic, see North (1990); Potter (1994), 146–58.
For the same palm-tree omen, see Plut. *Caes.* 47; Plutarch there also reports Livy's
account (from his lost Book 111) of an extraordinary piece of divination concerning
the battle – an equally dramatic departure from usual technique.

problem in anthropology, it is also a problem in literary criticism. The whole question of the kind of belief invited by different forms of speech and granted by different audiences is one that classicists have only quite recently begun to address, and this is particularly the case with texts that treat of religion: as Hunter says, 'in the realm of the presentation of the divine, . . . there is not even an agreed critical language with which to transcend unhelpful assertions about what poets did or did not "believe"'.[30]

The argument so far may appear to be no more than a new-fangled way of arriving at substantially the same conclusions as the old formalism, which saw Roman literature as isolated in its own sphere or spheres, unrelated to any real beliefs of either writers or audience, and floating over a fragmented culture which provided no bedrock of communal meaning. It is a mistake, however, to conclude that if we do not have one over-arching, integrating system we are left with nothing but cogs endlessly revolving without engaging.[31] Veyne's 'provinces' cannot be self-contained and independent, but must be given a foreign policy, allowing them to negotiate with and confront one another. They have their ambits defined, after all, and become apprehensible as such, precisely by virtue of their interaction with one another. Just as the theory of fiction sees this category being continually constituted and defined by the play with other forms of speech,[32] so too with each of the genres we group under the heading of Roman religion and literature. The co-existence of the genres of belief does not prove their impotence, but is rather the very condition that makes meaning possible. Meaning is produced by dialogue, at every level,[33] and the search for a single, monolithic meaning-system can only proceed at the expense of smothering this ubiquitous dialogic activity.[34] The rest of this chapter, and much of the rest of the book, will be devoted to analysing particular cases of these interactions, as we observe philosophy engaging with epic, satire with statuary, or lyric with sacrifice.

---

[30] Hunter (1992), 29 (on Callimachus and his peers). See Graf (1988); Feeney (1991), index s.v. 'belief/disbelief'; and the papers in Gill and Wiseman (1993).
[31] Martindale (1993b), 137.   [32] Feeney (1993a), 240–1.
[33] Martindale (1993a), 29–34.   [34] Kramer (1989), 114.

Belief in the Greeks

First, however, we need to uncover the usually hidden other half of the antithesis that conditions the normal modern image of a fragmented and enfeebled Roman culture. The problem of belief may appear to be a condition of a post-lapsarian state in which the Romans uniquely and unfortunately found themselves, but it is important to be explicit about what is at issue in the usual assumption that, whereas the Romans had balkanised brains, the Greeks (or the pre-Hellenistic Greeks) did not. This is not a book on Greek literature and Greek religion, so here I will do no more than is necessary for my purpose of keeping the Greek half of the inevitable antithesis out in the open (and we will be returning to this general area of concern from a rather different angle in the next chapter, 'Myth').

Veyne himself sees an important watershed in the Hellenistic age.[35] Still, as his own frequent comments on the pre-Hellenistic period show, the issue of plural modes of belief does not suddenly spring out of the sands of Alexandrian Egypt. To begin with, we may see plurality of modes of belief as a constitutive part of any self-conscious reflection upon the status of poetic speech. What was Stesichorus' audience supposed to 'believe' when he stood up and said, 'Actually, the story about Helen which the Muse and I gave you yesterday is not true – *this* one is' (fr. 192 *PMG*)? The problem of belief was always potentially in play, because the poets persistently put the issue of their authority and their fictive power in the foreground, and because the boundaries of credence are constituted by what one will not give credence to – there is no belief without disbelief.[36]

The poets' ways of talking about the gods were always multiple, and therefore always potentially in competition. There was no one frame of mind appropriate to the reception of all the varied forms of literature in which a Greek of the archaic or classical period might hear talk about the divine. Lamberton, speaking of the pre-Alexandrian period, highlights the fractured nature of the field we now label 'literature': 'Each preserved text had an identity of its own and a claim to truth, historic-

---

[35] Veyne (1988), 45.

[36] The folklorists Dégh and Vázsonyi (1976) discuss the volatility of the belief-criteria in the telling of legends; their conclusions are most apposite for ancient Greece, as Pratt (1993), 36 points out.

ity, or beauty that was unique and not easily compared with the claims of other texts . . . Homer . . . remained a discrete category of experience to a degree that may be difficult for us to appreciate, and an under-standing of Homer – of *what* as well as *how* the *Iliad* and *Odyssey* communicated – could not easily be compared to the understanding of other literature.'[37] 'Believing in' what you heard in Homer was not the same experience as 'believing in' what you heard in Alcaeus or saw in Aeschylus.

If literature was always a fragmented field, then literature's overlap with non-literary contexts (themselves not categorisable under any one heading) is also problematic as far back as one can go in Greek literary history. There was no age of Kronos when literarity was not a problem, when belief in 'art' and belief in 'religion' cohered in a perfect mesh, when one frame of mind could carry you over from a non-literary context to a literary one and then back again. The majority of Hellenists, however, do appear to believe that such a Golden Age once existed among the Greeks. The usual hypothesis – founded ultimately in Ro-manticism, and grounded recently in structuralism and cultural and symbolic anthropology – would have it that there was indeed an inherent unity pervading the mental experience of the *polis*. According to Bruit Zaidman and Schmitt Pantel, for example, 'the two aspects of Greek religion that we have described successively in this book – the cultic practices . . . and the systems for representing the divine . . . – have to be conceptualized and interpreted as a unified totality'.[38]

Yet this organicism is open to serious objections. It is by no means clear that we may view any culture as 'a historically constructed system of cognition which is coherent, all-encompassing and non-individual'.[39] At a more fundamental level, even basic semiotics tells us that any experi-ence, including religious experience, must be contextualised. Encounter-ing a god in a temple is not the same as encountering a god in a book or a song: 'Greek divinities do not have "essences" . . . they must be placed in

---

[37] Lamberton (1986), 11 (original emphasis); cf. Parker (1983), 15–16, on the import-ance of genre-differences for the student of classical Greek religion. On fictionality in early Greek literature, see Bowie (1993) and Pratt (1993).

[38] Bruit Zaidman and Schmitt Pantel (1992), 228.

[39] Bloch (1989), 106–36 (quotation from 109); cf. Desan (1988), 64–5. See Osborne (1993) for objections to the instinctive search for homology between the religious and political spheres in Greece.

the context which determines their divine personalities'.[40] The most sustained recent attempt to be precise about the contextualisation of divine personalities may be found in Mikalson's book on religion and Attic tragedy, in which he argues against the assumption that the Olympian deities like Zeus and Athena were 'believed in' or 'worshipped' in a form that overlapped with their representation on the tragic stage.[41] To take an example from a rather different sphere, Hamilton's study of the literary and iconographic evidence for the Athenian festival of the Anthesteria ends up concentrating on the 'disjunction between text and image'. Each medium has its own priorities and interests, and its own semiotics, so that the representation of sacrifice varies between the literary sources and the vases: 'the [literary] testimonia for the most part come from Greek drama, where the divine and public dominate; the vases seem to prefer the human to the divine, the generic to the specific, and the personal to the public'.[42] The contextual discrepancies which are so striking in the Roman cult of Bona Dea have their analogues in Greece as well.

Again, the conclusion for pre-Hellenistic Greece is not that all these 'theologies' are floating in the air and never engaging with one another, or that what we label as literature is less 'real' or significant – if I object to an aestheticised reading of Roman culture, the last thing I want to do is argue for an aestheticised reading of Greek culture. Mikalson's study, for example, is most successful in documenting the split between the representation of deities in cult and on the stage, but the main weakness in his approach is clearly that it depends ultimately upon the antithesis between 'literature' and 'real religion' that I called into question earlier.[43] The old-fashioned approach used to locate the quintessence of Athenian religion in their drama, but it only perpetuates the antithesis to reverse it and locate the quintessence of Athenian religion instead in a supposedly more real set of behaviours. Yunis is quite right to describe Mikalson's 'real religion' as an 'incoherent formulation'.[44] In Mikalson's usage, 'real religion' includes a range of practices that by no means constitute a single whole (civic cult, domestic cult, popular 'beliefs' which are identified with the kind of thing an orator felt was appropriate to say in

---

[40] Sourvinou-Inwood (1991), 5; cf. 147–50; Feeney (1991), 3–4, 45–7; Buxton (1994), 162–3.

[41] Mikalson (1991), following up his investigation of Athenian popular religion in Mikalson (1983). Similar arguments have been made in the case of Homer: Kirk (1990), 1–14.   [42] Hamilton (1992), 140.   [43] Above, pp. 1–2.

[44] Yunis (1993), 71.

public). In sum, there is no given 'real religion' which art is then varying or departing from, for what we label 'real religion' is itself a mobile set of discourses with varying degrees of overlap and competition. The field which modern scholars call 'Athenian religion' is that whole mobile set, with the addition of the overlapping and competing discourses we call 'literature'.[45]

Likewise, I am certainly not claiming that the Romans and Greeks of all periods and places were engaged with an identical set of problems as regards all these issues. There are powerful cultural transformations continually in train all over the diverse Greek world, from the beginning of the documented tradition down to the time when the Greeks were conquered by the Romans, and beyond, so that unlocalised generalisations about 'the Greek experience' are exceedingly problematic. For their part, the Romans, despite all their hellenisation, inhabited a different intellectual and cultural world even from their Greek contemporaries.[46] As someone primarily interested in investigating the cultural power of Roman religious discourses, I wish only to destabilise the prevalent casual assumption that Greece was uniquely privileged to an organic cultural unity of a kind denied to Rome (or modern society). This is the first step we must take if we are to resist being gulled into (as Hunter puts it when speaking of post-classical Greece) 'shutting off areas of meaning in the later text'.[47]

A Greek province of the brain

This detour through the Greek half of the antithesis also serves to highlight a major difference between the Greek and the Roman experience: the Greeks had no one to play for them the role they played for the Romans, while the Romans lived their entire experience in dialogue with this other culture.[48] Interaction with Greek culture was, from the start, a

---

[45] For more nuanced discussions of the disjunction between the mythical and ritualistic representation of a deity (Dionysus), see the papers of A. Henrichs and D. Obbink in Carpenter and Faraone (1993).   [46] Feeney (1991), 103–7.

[47] Hunter (1992), 33.

[48] Generally, on this process in archaic Rome, Momigliano (1989), esp. 110–12, Cornell (1995), 85–92, 118, 145–8; on religion in particular, North (1989), 578–80; Cornell (1995), 112, 161–3. Memorable pages on this topic in Norden (1939), 245–80, focusing on the illusions of finding a 'national', 'pre-Hellenising' moment in the Carmen Arvale. On the different nature of the Greek interaction with the Near East, see pp. 65–6 below.

distinctive feature of the Romans' relentlessly energetic modernism, marking them out from their peers as early as the seventh century BCE, when 'Rome, perhaps alone among the native communities of central Italy, began to take on some of the features of the Greek *polis*'.[49] Religion was as much involved in this process of cultural interaction as any other part of Roman life, and the Romans' religious dialogue with the Greek world was therefore very ancient. It was a dialogue that the Romans were careful never fully to naturalise or domesticate, maintaining throughout their history elaborate and self-conscious mechanisms for preserving a sense of distance and difference from the Greek element in their religious life (even if the distinctions they drew are not necessarily the same as those a modern historian might want to draw).[50]

Even under the monarchy Greek cults had found a home in the city (Hercules Invictus in the Forum Boarium), or had moulded Latin rites (Aventine Diana).[51] The early years of the Republic saw the introduction of Castor and Pollux (484 BCE) and Apollo (431 BCE); the Greek cult of Demeter, Iacchus, and Kore was the model for the cult of Ceres, Liber, and Libera established in 493 BCE.[52] Ceres and probably Apollo were introduced at the behest of the Sibylline oracles, Greek hexameter texts kept in the temple of Jupiter Capitolinus for consultation by a board of priests called the *decemuiri*, and in historical times these gods were worshipped (as was Hercules) *Achiuo ritu* or *Graeco ritu*, 'according to the Greek rite', in contrast to the 'ancestral rite', *patrius ritus* (Ceres was actually served by Greek priestesses from Campania).[53] Various features distinguished the Greek from the Roman rite, in particular the fact that

[49] Cornell (1995), 118; on the continuity of this cultural trait, Galinsky (1996), 332–50.

[50] Compare their self-consciousness about the foreignness of the Etruscan *haruspices* who participated in their civic cult, *Tusci ac barbari* according to the father of the Gracchi (Cic. *ND* 2. 11): North (1989), 583–4. These marginal individuals, or their low-class native equivalents, not any members of the priestly colleges, are the characters who are the butt of Cato's famous and so often misrepresented crack, that he could not understand how one *haruspex* could keep a straight face when he met another one (Cic. *Div.* 2.51; cf. Goar (1972), 39).

[51] Cornell (1995), 112, 162 (Hercules), 295 (Diana).

[52] Wissowa (1912), 268–71 (Castor and Pollux), 271–84 (Hercules), 293–5 (Apollo), 297–300 (Ceres); the dates are traditional, but the first century of the Republic is the right frame. This sketch glosses over the role of Phoenicians, Etruscans, and other Latins, and elides the distinctions between Greek cults brought in via neighbouring towns, or from Campania or Magna Graecia.

[53] See Cornell (1995), 263–4 for the antiquity of these features of Ceres' cult.

the Greeks sacrificed with the head bare or garlanded, the Romans with the head covered by a fold of the toga.[54] A Roman could tell at a glance, in other words, if a magistrate or priest was sacrificing to one of these imported deities.

Roman receptivity to importing Greek cult varied over time,[55] and the 'otherness' of the Greek element in the civic cult must likewise have been apprehended differently at different times by different people. Still, the categories of 'Greek' and 'Roman' were ones that citizens were used to negotiating, even as spectators of cult. The Greek component in public cult is not a novelty, not a distraction from what the Romans really or originally believed, but something carefully maintained as simultaneously integral and marginal, one of many ways of organising their apprehension of what they did and did not share with the world outside the city.

The interplay between Greek and Roman religion which is so familiar to readers of Roman literature is not, then, a self-contained game, but a mental capacity with analogues in centuries-long practice.[56] Our earliest texts show a delight in juxtaposing religious ideas from different registers, combining Homeric and cult epithets for Jupiter, or turning the epic hero Anchises into a proto-*decemuir* who consults sacred books.[57] Plautus puts on a bravura display with Mercury's prologue to the *Amphitryo*, enjoying the feat of throwing together 'Mercury' and 'Hermes', supposedly the 'same' at some level of comparison, yet scarcely reconcilable as figures of cult.[58] In the first line Mercury puns on the etymology of his Roman title (twenty lines before he actually speaks his name), showing his status as a god of *merc*antile activity (*mercimoniis*). He speaks as a business-man (or business-god) for seven lines before punning across into Greek to announce that he also has the messenger-function of the messenger-god Hermes (*nuntiis* and *nuntiem* in 8 and 9 look to the Greek ἑρμηνεύς which was the commonly accepted etymology for 'Hermes'): this move is anticipated at line 5 by his heavy stress on his power 'both abroad and at home' (*peregrique et domi*). He then claims that *both* activities have been allotted to him by the other gods (*nuntiis*

[54] Gagé (1955), 215–17.

[55] Garnsey and Saller (1987), 170; see below, pp. 51–2.

[56] Still fundamental is Fraenkel (1960; originally published in German in 1922), Ch. 3, and pp. 406–7.

[57] Feeney (1991), 111–12, on Anchises; 113 and 128 on the epithets.

[58] BNP, vol. 2 no. 2.1c.

praesim et lucro, 12). This mingling is highly diverting, characteristic of the 'wise guy', as Dumézil labels him here.[59] But Plautus is not 'carelessly and happily mingling', as Dumézil would have it. From the very start, Plautus is involving his audience in the difficult game of deciding who we are really looking at when we look at a figure on the stage during the *Amphitryo*. In the Prologue, we are made to wonder if the actor is representing the Hermes of the Greek original or the Mercury of the Latin adaptation, or both: soon we will be trying to decide if we are looking at Mercury or Sosia, Jupiter or Amphitryo. We even find ourselves involved in another related problem of category-judging as a result of Mercury's presence (50–63): what kind of play are we looking at? – a tragedy or a comedy (or a tragi-comedy)? The audience is involved in puzzling through various difficulties of categorisation, all introduced by one character revelling in his dual heritage. With an almost off-hand example of this suggestive complexity from comedy, one can only regret all the more bitterly the fragmentary nature of Ennius' *Annales*, in which multiple registers co-existed, but whose interaction we can no longer plot.

The ludi saeculares

Roman self-consciousness about the Greek component of civic cult did not disappear as time went on, but was always able to be activated. It provides a fascinating example of how self-conscious they could be about the contextual variability of their religious behaviour. As an example of this contextual variability, and as a way of focusing some of the main problems of talking about belief in a Roman context, it is worth looking in some detail at what is perhaps the most spectacular and systematic exploitation of the categories of Greek and Roman in cult, namely, the *ludi saeculares* staged by Augustus in 17 BCE.[60]

The first *ludi saeculares*, in 249 BCE, had been organised to expiate

---

[59] Dumézil (1970), 492. For an Ovidian exploitation of the mercantile-mythic split in Mercury's figure, see *Fast.* 5.663–92, with Miller (1991), 100–5.

[60] Pighi (1965) has texts, with discussion, of the *Commentarium* (*CIL* 6. 32323; *ILS* 5050) and of the Sibylline oracle (*FGH* 257 F 37); BNP, vol. 2, no. 5.7b. On the Ludi Saeculares in general, see Nilsson (1920); on Augustus', see Price in BNP, vol. 1, Ch. 4; Galinsky (1996), 100–6.

prodigies after the Sibylline books had been consulted by the *decemuiri*, the board of ten priests who supervised the Sibylline oracles and foreign cults in general.[61] Accordingly, in the *ludi* of 249 there was a markedly Greek stamp to the two deities honoured with three successive nocturnal sacrifices performed *Achiuo ritu*, 'according to the Greek rite' – Dis Pater (that is, Dives Pater, 'wealthy father', a calque for the Greek god of the underworld, Pluto, 'Wealth'), and his bride Proserpina (Persephone). Neither of these had cult in the city, and it was the first time that the state had honoured these gods of the underworld. Augustus' *ludi* some 230 years later were organised by the same board of priests responsible for foreign cult (though now fifteen in number, hence *quindecimuiri*). Augustus was himself a member of this panel, and oversaw the production of the Sibylline oracle which prescribed the occasion and the form for the *ludi*; these Greek hexameter texts, traditionally under the care of the *quindecimuiri*, had recently been purged and transferred from the temple of Jupiter Optimus Maximus to the temple of Apollo Palatinus, part of Augustus' residential complex.[62]

Augustus transformed the atmosphere and purpose of the *ludi*, orientating them away from infernal expiation towards future fecundity,[63] but the ritual still lay within the purview of the *quindecimuiri*, and Augustus retained the importance of a Greek component, even throwing it into relief with an intricately contrapuntal patterning of night- and day-time activities. There were still three successive night-time sacrifices, beginning with the night of 31 May, at the same site in the Campus Martius as before, performed – *Achiuo ritu* – by Augustus: the emperor probably sacrificed in Greek dress on the first night, and then, at all the succeeding ceremonies, in the toga, but with bare head in the Greek manner.[64] The underworld deities of 249 BCE, Dis Pater and Proserpina, yielded place to three more beneficent honorands, who nonetheless shared with Dis Pater and Proserpina the twin characteristics of being Greek in nomenclature and without cult in the Roman state: Moerae, 'Fates'; Ilithyiae, 'Deities of Childbirth'; and Terra Mater, 'Earth Mother', the Γαῖα of the oracle, but sounding like the Greek Δημήτηρ (and not, be it noted,

[61] Latte (1960), 246–8.
[62] The date of transfer is guaranteed by Tib. 2.5.17–18 and Virg. *Aen.* 6.72: Smith (1913), 444.   [63] Nilsson (1920), 1716.
[64] Turcan (1988), 2.9, on the evidence for Domitian in 88 CE.

Tellus, the name of Earth in civic cult).[65] Set against these doubly Greek nocturnal rites were three successive day-time sacrifices, performed by Augustus and Agrippa together, still *Achiuo ritu*, but this time in honour of Jupiter Optimus Maximus, the supreme Roman god and centre of Republican cult (1 June), then Juno Regina, his Capitoline consort (2 June), followed by Apollo and Diana on the Palatine (3 June), inhabitants of the Augustan temple dedicated only ten and a half years previously.

We have here an extraordinarily sharp set of demarcations: night/day, without/with civic cult, Greek/Roman, aniconic/iconic, personifications/individuals, un-Olympian/Olympian, chthonic/heavenly, outside/inside the *pomerium*, plain/hilltop, single/paired sacrificer. The arrangement of the sacrifices shows the *princeps* flaunting the ability of his state, his family, and himself to dominate and control the greatest possible range of religious meaning and power, as he draws alien entities of birth and fecundity into the same ring as the ancient gods of the Roman Capitol, staging a pageant which probes the boundaries between the Roman state and the *oikoumene*. Augustus and his colleagues have condensed into one sequence the dynamic interplay between Greek and Roman categories that had served the state so well for so long.

These three days must have been among the most significant in Augustus' life, yet as soon as we start talking about 'personal belief' the structure that generates that significance falls apart in our hands. Augustus will have sacrificed to Jupiter Optimus Maximus many times before, yet he was the first person ever to sacrifice to the Moerae in the city of Rome, and no other Roman sacrificed to them again for sixty-three years, when Augustus' great-nephew Claudius next staged the *ludi saeculares*. Does this mean that Augustus and the many thousands of spectators believed in what he was doing during the first day-time rite, because it was Roman and traditional, but not in what he was doing during the first night-time rite, because it was Greek and unprecedented? Even to pose the question in these terms is to reveal its futility. It is precisely the intersection between the Roman and the Greek, the ancient and the novel, that generates the cognitive and emotional power of the three days. The rite as a whole articulates with remarkable economy that

---

[65] Latte (1960), 299, on the absence of these deities from Roman cult. On the strong links in Greece between Moirai and Eileithyiae, see Roscher (1884–1937), 2.2.3091.

theme of rebirth within a reworked traditional framework which is the hallmark of the Augustan New Age ideology, and, indeed, of the régime as a whole.[66] The negotiation between the novel and the traditional is central to the exercise, and the apparatus is smashed if we concentrate on the novelty as an inorganic and less meaningful element, or worry away at which bit of the pageant meant more than the rest.

The rite comes clothed with an aura of tradition, but it is just as easy to apprehend it as revolutionary.[67] The final recipient of sacrifice, Apollo, the only Greek-named deity honoured in day-time, is as interesting a compound of the novel and the traditional as his protégé, Augustus. He had been established in the city for 400 years, but now he had a new temple and persona, living within the *pomerium* for the first time, and encroaching on the prerogatives of his father Jupiter. If we look at the distribution of offerings with Apollo in mind, we see interesting lines of connection being set up across the apparently stark dichotomies of the rite. Augustus alone at night sacrificed nine female lambs and nine female kids to the Moerae, and a pregnant sow to Terra Mater, while Augustus and Agrippa together in the day each sacrificed a bull and a cow to Jupiter and Juno respectively. To the Ilithyiae Augustus offered twenty-seven cakes, divided into three categories (two of them transliterated Greek words, *popana* and *phthoes*); most remarkably, since (so far as we know) Apollo had never received bloodless sacrifice in Rome before,[68] Augustus and Agrippa offered the same to Apollo and the same to Diana. The choice of offerings cuts across the gulf of night and day, establishing Apollo and his sister as the mediators between the two categories of the pageant. Apollo's host and protégé, Augustus, likewise becomes the mediator between the epochs, cults and cultures of the *ludi*. The *quindecimuiri* had oversight of all foreign cults, in particular Apollo and the Magna Mater, the deities whose residences flanked Augustus' own; by Augustus' organisation, Jupiter and Juno have been, as it were, subsumed into the *Graecus ritus* of the whole pageant and of Apollo Palatinus in particular.[69]

---

[66] Zanker (1988), 49–53, on the new *regnum* of Apollo. As soon as the inscription was discovered, Mommsen (1905) immediately saw this interstitial character of the rite as crucial; cf. Nilsson (1920), 1717.

[67] Again, see Mommsen (1905), e.g., 356, on the revolutionary import of praying for the Roman people and the legions as separate entities.   [68] Gagé (1955), 631–2.

[69] Gagé (1955), 635–7.

The carmen saeculare

In the Sibylline oracle's prescriptions for the *ludi* (18–22), following the itemising of the sacrifices are prescriptions for paeans sung in Latin (ἀειδόμενοί τε Λατῖνοι/παιᾶνες), performed by youths and maidens, all with their parents still living, in separate choruses. The *Acta* record that a *carmen* was sung twice on the last day, first before Apollo Palatinus and then before Jupiter Optimus Maximus. It was sung by twin choruses of twenty-seven boys and twenty-seven girls with parents still living (one boy for each of the cakes given to Apollo and one girl for each of the cakes given to Diana). The *Acta* further record: *carmen composuit Q. Horatius Flaccus* ('the hymn was composed by Q. Horatius Flaccus'). This *carmen* of course survives in Horace's corpus, as the *Carmen Saeculare*, and in it we may trace a poetic engagement with the ritual categories so carefully built and rebuilt by the *princeps*. If the *ludi* themselves illuminate how self-consciously the Romans could manipulate different contexts and categories in their cult, the distinctive discourse of the *carmen* adds another dimension to that self-examination.

Horace's *carmen* acknowledges the night/day distinctions of the sacrifices, grouping the three foreign night-time deities in sequence (13–32) and speaking of 'games crowded three times in bright day and as many times in pleasing night' (*ludos | ter die claro totiensque grata | nocte frequentis*, 22–4). From the beginning, however, the hymn concentrates on following up the ritual's use of Apollo and Diana as a bridge across the categories, affirming more openly than the ritual itself their status as the end aimed at by the trajectory of the whole three days.[70] The *carmen* begins with an invocation of the Palatine pair: *Phoebe siluarumque potens Diana, | lucidum caeli decus* ('Phoebus, and Diana with dominion over woods, shining adornment of heaven'). This language already collapses the night/day distinction, for the singular phrase 'shining adornment of heaven' refers jointly to the pair, the brother shining as the sun at day and the sister as the moon at night. The second stanza, referring to the fact that the *carmen* is being sung at the command of the Sibylline verses, glances at the new role of Apollo as the custodian of those verses. The third stanza catches at another new role of Apollo when the choruses turn to Sol, the Sun, saying that he is born 'another

[70] Gagé (1955), 635.

and the same', *alius . . . et idem* (10). These words allude not only to the physical illusion that the sun is 'another' sun at each new day, but also to the 'otherness and sameness' of Apollo's syncretism with Sol/Helios. In the oracle, Apollo is likewise named as 'the one who is also called Helios' (ὅστε καί Ἥλιος κικλήσκεται, 17); we must remind ourselves that when the choruses first sang they were facing the temple of Apollo Palatinus, on whose roof stood a representation of the chariot of the Sun, to which the choruses point at the beginning of this stanza, with the words *curru nitido*, 'shining chariot' (9).[71]

After these first three stanzas concerned with the Palatine pair in one manifestation or another, the choruses address Ilithyia, the goddess of childbirth. The movement of the *carmen* uses this ordering to establish the links between Ilithyia and Apollo and Diana that Augustus had established by choice of sacrificial offering. A further connection across these categories is forged when Horace uses 'Lucina' as a possible title for Ilithyia (15), reminding us that Diana herself could be regarded as Lucina, controlling the same sphere as Ilithyia. Prayers to the Fates and Earth follow (25–32), before the choruses once more return to Apollo, mild and calm as in the Palatine cult statue, and Diana (as Luna, 36).

We are now half-way through the *carmen* and there has not yet been any mention of the Roman deities who received sacrifice on the first and second days, Jupiter and Juno; this sense of exclusion is strengthened by the closural force of the address to Apollo and Diana in 33–6, for that address takes us back, by ring-composition, to their initial invocation in the first stanza.[72] Since the discovery of the *Acta* in 1890 it has been clear that Jupiter and Juno must be the gods now addressed as the *carmen* turns at the half-way point (*Roma si uestrum est opus . . .* , 'if Rome is your business...', 37), for the next three stanzas lead up to a description of Augustus sacrificing to these addressees with white oxen (49), and the *Acta* make it plain that Jupiter and Juno were the only gods who received such offerings during the *ludi*.[73] But – in an elision which is practically unthinkable in a hymn, where the proper naming of the invoked deity was considered vital – Jupiter and Juno are not named as they are addressed. Hence the universal assumption amongst commentators before 1890 that this entire section was likewise addressed to Apollo

[71] Hardie (1993b), 125–6.   [72] As Richard Tarrant points out to me.
[73] Mommsen (1905), 357–8.

and Diana. The Sibylline oracle, which until 1890 had been the only evidence for the form of the rite, states explicitly that Apollo should receive the same bovine sacrificial offerings as Jupiter and Juno (16–18): only the discovery of the *Acta* revealed that there had been a change of plan, and that Apollo had in fact received the same offerings as the Ilithyiae. With only the misleading evidence of the Sibylline oracle to go by, and without any explicit mention of a change in addressee, the white oxen mentioned by Horace in line 49 would inevitably be taken to refer to Apollo's sacrifices.

Jupiter and Juno are not named, then, although the choruses are now directly addressing them. With this dramatic omission, Horace alludes to and corrects the suppression of the names of Apollo and Diana at the beginning of Virgil's *Georgics*, where Apollo and Diana are invoked anonymously as 'the extremely bright lights of the universe' (*clarissima mundi*|*lumina*, 1.5–6);[74] throughout the hymn, Horace compensates abundantly for that suppression, parading one name after another for Apollo and his sister (Phoebus, Sol, Apollo; Diana, Lucina, Luna). Juno in fact is never named at all in the course of the *carmen*, and Jupiter (apart from brief mention as the sky-god in 32, *Iouis aurae*) finds his way only into the last stanza, where he does no more than approve the favourable response of Apollo and Diana, whose praises close the hymn (*doctus et Phoebi chorus et Dianae* | *dicere laudes*, 75–6). It is hard to know whether this suppression of Jupiter and Juno would have been more striking during the first performance of the hymn in front of Apollo Palatinus, or during the second performance in front of Jupiter Capitolinus. The eclipse of the old Capitoline deities by the Palatine gods of the *princeps* is most remarkable, and it has been exposed more nakedly in ten minutes of singing than it had been in three days of ritual action. And as the *carmen* progresses on its career in Horace's lyric corpus, leaving further and further behind the ritual context which makes it possible to glimpse Jupiter and Juno as the addressees here, it paradoxically stresses more and more powerfully the ritual's suppression of the Capitoline deities in favour of the Palatine pair.

The paean is by origin a hymn to Apollo and Artemis,[75] and Horace's hymn, as the paean called for by the Sibylline oracle, is capitalising on

[74] As Richard Thomas points out to me.
[75] Procl. *Chr.* in Phot. *Bibl.* 320a21 (my thanks to A. Barchiesi for this point). In *C.* 4.6.37–8, Horace refers to the *Carmen Saeculare* as a hymn to Apollo and Diana.

this ancient formal feature in order to reinforce the ritual's emphasis on the Palatine pair. If the *carmen* exaggerates this theme of the ritual, however, in other ways it represents not an exaggeration but a departure. In particular, its way of naming the Greek deities who received night-time sacrifice is an interesting variation upon Augustus' emphases.[76]

In line 14, Ilithyia is addressed with her Greek title, for which there was no exact Latin equivalent, but Horace immediately presses the alternative naming style of hymns into novel service when he goes on to say *siue tu Lucina probas uocari | seu Genitalis* ('whether you prefer to be called Lucina or Genitalis', 15–16). Here he offers the Greek goddess 'a choice between two Latin cult names, *Lucina* and *Genitalis*: "Ilithyia – shall we (in Latin) call you Lucina or Genitalis?"'[77] The renaming of the alien divinity, hitherto outside the cult of the *res publica*, is strongly marked, for her unprecedented function is now to assist the success of Augustus' marriage legislation. It is in order to highlight the stresses of this cultural transference that Horace in the next stanza turns to another world of language altogether, with his notorious evocation of Latin constitutional jargon, so often dismissed as a mere blunder: *patrum . . . | decreta super iugandis | feminis* ('the decrees of the fathers concerning the yoking of women', 17–19). The next Greek deities invoked are the Moerae. They are Latinised as *Parcae* (25), with another Latin equivalent for their Greek name, *fata*, also placed emphatically as the last word of their stanza (28). Finally, Augustus had sacrificed to 'Earth' under the name *Terra Mater*, deliberately choosing a title which was not part of the state religion, but Horace chooses instead the word *Tellus* (29), which was the name of Earth in civic cult; he reinforces the link with the 'Earth' of civic cult by associating Tellus with Ceres (29–30), for Ceres' statue stood outside the temple of Tellus.[78]

In rewriting the Greek nomenclature used by the *princeps*, the Grecising hymn is more concerned to establish a Latin atmosphere than is the state ritual itself. If we are to read off 'degree of authenticity of belief' against a scale of Latinity or Romanness, we will end up saying that the *carmen* is more 'authentic' than the ritual, at which point we may well conclude that we are not using helpful terminology. Instead, we might see the *carmen* as engaging with the dynamics of the ritual, not replicat-

[76] McDermott (1981), 1665.

[77] McDermott (1981), 1665, n.71; Bentley's emendation to the Greek *Genetyllis* destroys this point.　　　[78] Plin. *HN* 34.15; cf. Ov. *Fast.* 1.671–3.

ing them, but setting up a tangentially related set of categories and perspectives for the audience to manipulate as they are challenged to use the *carmen* as a way of looking back over the last three days and forward over the next one hundred and ten years.

Augustus' pageant is a semiotic system of the utmost intricacy, and Horace's *carmen* does not – indeed, can not – reflect or re-embody it. By altering emphases and collapsing distinctions as well as observing them, the *carmen* insistently calls attention to the fact that it is not the rite, that it is not tautologous. It accomplishes this, above all, by marking out a space for poetry as a distinctive discourse. The thorough Latinising of the deities addressed is a sign of this ambition, as is the way the *carmen* looks forward to its reception as a further piece of Horatian lyric.[79] More significant still is the dialogue with the *Aeneid* of Virgil, dead not two years before. Throughout, the *carmen* is acknowledging the fact that the *Aeneid* has already become the cardinal medium for conceptualising the new ideology.[80] Further, Horace depicts the present actions of Augustus as the fulfilment of the text of the *Aeneid*. Augustus is 'superior to the one waging war, gentle to the prostrate enemy' (*bellante prior, iacentem | lenis in hostem*, 51–2), and his empire is world-wide (53–6). Augustus has here become the subject and the addressee of Anchises' prophecy in *Aeneid* 6, which had prophesied world dominion for Augustus (6.792–800), and which had itself become a Sibylline oracle at the end. When Anchises turns to the 'Roman', and commands him 'do you, Roman, remember | . . . to spare the conquered and war down the proud' (*tu . . . Romane, memento | . . . parcere subiectis et debellare superbos*, 6.851–3), he is using Sibylline language of the same kind used by the Sibylline oracle for the *ludi saeculares*: 'remember, Roman' (μεμνῆσθαι, ᾽Ρωμαῖε, 3). The poetic prophecy of a predecessor has here become more than a text to be alluded to: its oracular Sibylline power is now reanimated. Horace's chorus makes the Latin hexameters of Virgil collaborate with the Greek hexameters of Augustus' Sibylline oracle, which is an instrument and cause of ritual, but also, after all, a poetic text of a certain kind in its own right. Our categories of poetry and ritual break down as the *carmen* tells us that both Virgil's and Augustus' Sibylline oracles have made this 'happen'.

One of poetry's distinctive powers is its capacity to outstrip time, and

---

[79] Barchiesi (1996), 8–9.   [80] Fraenkel (1957), 375.

Horace's long-standing obsession with this topic is in play here. Horace believes that his poetry can celebrate and preserve memory more power-fully than other media, more powerfully than marble or bronze monu-ments;[81] the Horatian motif acquires extra power in this ritual context, for the state itself is concerned to preserve the memory of the *ludi*, with seven lines of the inscription devoted to a *senatus consultum* ordering the erection of two monuments, in bronze and marble, for the future mem-ory of the event (*ad futuram rei memoriam*, lines 58–63). In the *carmen*, Horace is celebrating and preserving a particular moment of sacred time (*tempore sacro*, 4), and his characteristic lyric interest in that function is especially charged, for the *ludi* are themselves all about time. Their preservative ritual is designed to create a new cycle of time, a perma-nence for the state that transcends any individual's lifetime: the *Acta* twice refer to the fact that no one will again see this ritual, that no mortal may see the games twice (lines 54–6). Horace's lyric obsession with transience and permanence is in a novel dialogue with the ritual's obsess-ion with transience and permanence, and with the state's attempts in bronze and marble to preserve the memory of that ritual.[82]

The *carmen*'s self-consciousness about the fact that it is a poem, and cannot be co-extensive with the rite, is obliquely reflected in the interest modern scholars show in debating whether or not it was 'part of' the rite. In some senses it was (it had been prescribed by the Sibylline verses, and its singing was commemorated on the inscribed *Acta*);[83] in some senses it was not (it was not a *precatio*, 'cult prayer', strictly speaking, and its actual words were not engraved on the marble as were the words of Augustus' and Agrippa's *precationes*).[84] The odd position of the *carmen* within the rite is not a gaffe, but a sophisticated acknowledgment of its nuanced relationship with the rest of the proceedings. As we shall see in Chapter 4, 'Ritual', one of the most important contributions from the

---

[81] Putnam (1986), esp. 300–6; Hardie (1993b); Barchiesi (1996), 18–22.

[82] In *C.* 4.6.44 Horace mentions his name for the only time in the *Odes*; in a poem about the performance of the *carmen saeculare*, this citation clearly alludes to the commemoration of his name on the inscription; but it is significant that he rein-scribes that commemoration into the future speech of one of the girls of the chorus, once again stressing the superiority of his own genre.

[83] Cairns (1992b), 29 n.92.

[84] Scheid (1993), 113. Interestingly, the words of the new *carmen* for Septimius Severus' games of 204 CE were engraved in the *Acta*: Pighi (1965), 165–6 (fr. Va, 60–71).

revisionist studies of Roman religion has been the recognition that exegesis and interpretative dialogue help constitute Roman religious practice, rather than being something extraneous or added on.[85] The *carmen* and the *ludi*, independent yet mutually implicated, are our clearest test case. Interpretation is already explicitly a part of the whole three-day spectacle.

Belief in performance

However persuasive or unpersuasive readers may find the preceding argument about the limitations of 'belief' as a category for analysing the *ludi* and the *carmen*, it may be objected that I am devoting a good deal of space to a poem which is wholly untypical. For a hundred years, after all, we have had incontrovertible evidence that this poem was actually performed as part of state-organised cult, whereas there is no single other poem surviving in the Latin canon of which the same can be said with certainty. Faced with the problem of how to read other poems that take the form of hymns or prayers (Catullus 34 or Propertius 4.6, for example), some Latinists have argued that these poems were in fact 'really performed', and in a cult context;[86] the response has usually been to reassert that these poems are a 'literary exercise, rather than a genuine hymn'.[87] Such a polarisation is very pervasive. It lies, for example, behind Fraenkel's desire to remove the *carmen saeculare* from being 'part of' the rite. He wishes to see the *carmen* as a truly – quintessentially – Horatian poem, whose status as such would be compromised if it were seen as one of a series of cult actions.[88]

The important question to ask at the outset is not whether a particular Latin hymn was really performed, but rather what is at stake in asking that question. Making the Latin hymn look more like a Greek one is usually the answer. We need once again, therefore, to bring out into the open the way in which the terms of debate are being set by the unspoken Greek half of the antithesis. The assumption is that Greek hymns of the pre-Hellenistic period were actually performed in a genuinely religious or cultic setting, and commanded a corresponding degree of belief, so that if we want to make Roman hymns serious we will assimilate them to

---

[85] Below, pp. 127–33.   [86] Wiseman (1985), 96–9; Cairns (1984).
[87] Zetzel (1992), 98.   [88] Fraenkel (1957), 378–82.

this model as much as possible, while if we want to stress their belated and artificial nature we will distance them from this model as much as possible.

In fact, however, remarkably few of the hymns surviving from the canon of pre-Hellenistic times were definitely composed for initial 'real' performance in a cult context, and the genuine examples of cult hymns can represent a low level of endeavour.[89] The Homeric Hymns, with the possible exception of *Delian Apollo*, were almost certainly not composed for cult performance in honour of their addressees; nor were the surviving hymns of Alcaeus or Sappho.[90] We do not know the context for Alcaeus' hymn to Hermes, for example, but when he begins by hailing the god and saying that he is singing of him because that is what he feels like (χαῖρε, . . . σὲ γάρ μοι | θῦμος ὕμνην, 308b. 1–2), he is using the language not of cult-song but of the rhapsodic *prooemium*.[91]

From the earliest times, Greek poets had been using the hymn form 'as a vehicle for a literary fictional occasion',[92] a point of departure for all kinds of experiment in the realms of representation and cult. A fine example is to be found in Alcaeus' *Hymn to Apollo*, in which the poet (with pride, arrogance, or glee?) introduces to his audience an Apollo who 'is not his own Apollo, but a stranger to the cult of his native land and neighbourhood'.[93] Individual performers such as Alcaeus or the poet of the Homeric Hymn were necessarily in an oblique and distanced relationship to the choruses who were the typical singers of archaic and classical cult songs such as paeans and dithyrambs.[94] Even in the case of performed choral cult song the problems of representation are not conjured away, if only because 'performance . . . is itself an enactment of something further (religious belief or civic ideology), and thus itself a "text" to be interpreted'.[95] The question of a performed choral song's 'reality' can itself be energised by the odd status of the voice of its individual composer, who is at one with the song in a sense (even if not

---

[89] Campbell (1983), 149–50; Bremer (1981), 203.

[90] Bulloch (1985), 7, in general; cf. Bremer (1981), 213; Parker (1991), 1–2 (Homeric Hymns); Page (1955), 16–17, 42–3 (Sappho), 244, 247, 271 (Alcaeus); Burnett (1983), 6, 229 (Lesbian hymns). On the Romanticising urge to find an authenticating cult context for Lesbian poetry in general, see Feeney (1993b), 55–6.

[91] Page (1955), 254 n.5.   [92] Bulloch (1985), 7; cf. Williams (1968), 156–7.

[93] Page (1955), 247; cf. 271 on Eros.   [94] Cairns (1984), 139.

[95] Kennedy (1993), 22.

necessarily jointly performing or even present), and whose status will guarantee the posterity of the song after the particular performance.[96] Even more radically, Mary Depew suggests that the 'deictic markers' of hymns (all the linguistic features that draw attention to the 'here', the 'now', and the 'I' of a celebratory occasion) loosen the ties between performed discourse and its context, objectifying the performance of an utterance, making it potentially into a text.[97] Such self-awareness about the posterior fate of the song is crucial: interpretation continued outside any cult or performance context, for the song-scripts were copied, re-read, and re-performed outside the original context (otherwise, obviously, we would not have them).[98]

In considering Roman poems in this tradition, then, 'real performance' is not the trump card its advocates take it to be. The 'reality' proves impossible to ground, and the assumptions of cultural homogeneity entailed by the word 'performance' are problematic, even in the Greek world which is held up as the ideal model: auditors and readers of 'hymns' in Greece had been negotiating the problems of representation and context since the archaic period. Various performance contexts for Hellenistic and Roman hymns are certainly possible, and the conventional antitheses between pre-Classical and post-Classical conditions in this regard have no doubt been much overstated;[99] but the crucial point is that there is no straight line from a performance context to the solution of the problems of belief, authenticity or social function.

Hymns in books

If language of 'real performance' appears to be a less reliable tool than one might have hoped, we still face the problem of how to read the Roman hymns. On the basis of the general argument so far, we may grant that our modern dichotomies between genuine belief and scepti-

[96] Morgan (1993).
[97] I reproduce here the phrasing of the précis of Depew's important paper, 'Greek Hymn: Representing the poet and the community', forthcoming in *Matrices of Genre: Authors, Canons and Society* (Cambridge, Mass.).
[98] Cairns (1984), 150. It has been claimed that archaic lyric was transmitted solely by means of continual re-performance (e.g. Herington (1985), esp. 48–50). But this flies in the face even of arithmetic: Alcaeus and Sappho were monumental authors, who each wrote more poetry than Catullus, Propertius and Tibullus *put together*.
[99] Cameron (1995), 64–70.

cism will not be helpful. The problem of belief in the Greek world was always changing, and we may point to various crucial stages at which the terms of debate shifted radically (with the 'invention' of science, philosophy, or mythography); but it is a fantasy to posit a pre-Hellenistic era when 'belief' was not problematic, and a post-Classical era when 'scepticism' was total.

Not helpful, either, are our dichotomies between 'religious' and 'secular'. The closest ancient approximation to this kind of language in our context is the distinction drawn, from Plato on, between songs addressed to gods and songs addressed to human beings. This, however, is fundamentally a rhetorical distinction, not one based on belief or emotion or even occasion.[100] The word 'religious' does not correspond to an ancient category, so that there is no already existing entity, 'religion', to be used as a yardstick for measuring a hymn's success or failure.[101] Hunter, in discussing the differences between a hymn of Callimachus and an aretalogy of Isis, is quite right to suggest 'non-literary/literary' as a more useful category distinction than 'religious/secular' (or, one might add, 'religious/literary').[102] This brings us to the nub of the problem, for we need to ask why 'literary' is a term of disparagement amongst Classicist literary critics. The challenge is to put the right adverb in front of the word 'literary': not 'merely', but 'distinctively'.

Any hymn by a Roman author is simultaneously in dialogue both with its literary tradition and with many other earlier and contemporary religious discourses: the religious monuments of the city, the philosophy of Stoics or Epicureans, the rituals of sacrifice and libation, to name only the most obvious. We must give full force to these other religious discourses in our interpretation, yet the danger of this richer cultural contextualisation is that it can blot out the special status of conversations with the literary tradition, which provided the forms and models of hymnic language. The hymns known to Propertius or Horace were the often anonymous productions sung on cult occasions in the contemporary Greek world (at best undistinguished and at worst doggerel), together with the counterparts of these Greek hymns in Rome – and, in addition, the splendid artefacts preserved in the literary corpus under the

[100] Harvey (1955), 159, 165–9.
[101] Cf. Henrichs (1993), 127 n.1, in connection with Callimachus' *Hymns*, on the error of treating 'the poet's "religion"' as if it were an autonomous entity separate from his poetics'.   [102] Hunter (1992), 29.

names of Pindar, Alcaeus, Callimachus and the rest.[103] For the Roman poets, as for Callimachus, entering into a dialogue with their predecessors would have been a far more attractive and important cultural project than reproducing the material of contemporary cult, for they did not have the nostalgia for doggerel that we do: once again, Horace's *carmen saeculare* is proof of how untempting the evocation of quotidian cult song could be for a Roman poet and audience, and how strong the urge to maintain a space for poetry could be even in the context of state ritual.

The *non sequitur* which commonly handicaps discussion at this point is the idea that this cultural project of dialogue with the tradition takes place 'in a social and intellectual vacuum'.[104] Yet, quite apart from the fact that this vacuum was in fact a very full one at Rome, crammed with many other religious representations and arguments, it would be strange to think that it was not a serious endeavour for Roman poets and their audience to process this immensely authoritative corpus, to engage in a dialogue with it, to tease out the differences and similarities, and to use the distance it provided as a way of focalising contemporary concerns, reflecting upon the differences so as to home in on what makes 'our' situation unique.[105] The fact that this dialogue may not be taking place in a ritual or performative context does not derogate from the cultural work it is doing. An analogy with the Mass of our modern musical tradition may be helpful.[106] From Bach's B Minor Mass onwards, the musical Mass is not necessarily liturgical or sacramental, by virtue of its length, alternative musical structures, and recapitulation of earlier portions of the liturgy out of order. Despite these liturgical licences, which make them incompatible with church performance, the Masses are still 'religious' in some worthwhile sense of the word, and it would be odd to dismiss them as merely parasitical upon the sung liturgical mass, with which they continue to engage even centuries after diverging. Chastising

---

[103] Norden (1913), 160 and (1939), 251, for this point. On the Greek hymns, see also Wilamowitz's note in Norden (1913), 392, and Cairns (1992b), 13. On the Roman hymns, Norden (1939), esp. 274–5.

[104] Hunter (1992), 29; cf. 33, and Bing (1988), 26 n.38.

[105] For fine recent studies of Callimachus' *Hymns* in this connection, see Hunter (1992), Bing (1993), and the papers of C. Calame, M. Depew, M.W. Haslam and A. Henrichs in Harder-Regtuit-Wakker (1993).

[106] My thanks to Susanne Wofford for suggesting this analogy, and to Larry Earp of the University of Wisconsin School of Music for discussing it with me.

Horace for composing a hymn that was not part of cult is like chastising
Beethoven for composing a Mass that was not part of cult; and trying to
recuperate an Horatian hymn by saying it might have been performed
beside an altar is like trying to recuperate Beethoven's Mass by saying it
might have been performed in a church.

The absence of a context, or the difference between contexts, so far
from being a scandal to interpretation, will often be the point. Catullus'
weirdly context-less Poem 34 (*Dianae sumus in fide*), phenomenally
successful at capturing a nostalgic atmosphere of archaising piety, yet
devoid of clues to date and occasion, may be read alongside other poems
of his in which the problem of context appears to be the main point at
issue.[107] Thirty years later, however, Horace rewrote the hymn so that it
was saturated with context. His *C.* 1.21 is still a hymn to Diana, still with
her name as the first word, but Catullus' words have been transformed
into an icon of Augustus' revolutionary Apollo Palatinus, with Diana,
together with her mother, now one of a pair, flanking Apollo, as in the
statuary of the temple. There are many other forms of experience in play
here – the temple, its statues, the festivities outside it. Yet Horace's
elaborate instructions to the non-existent choruses of boys and girls
foreground the poet's own power as not just the stage-manager but the
literal creator of the entire 'event';[108] and the prayer which these choruses
are instructed to sing at the end (*uestra . . . prece*, in the last line) is not
co-extensive with the poem itself. The poem remains determinedly a
poem, part of its tradition: its main energy comes from its recreation of
Catullus in a new context, no longer Italian and Republican, but global
and Imperial. Diana, by Horace's construction, was headed for the
Palatine all the time, just as Catullus' poem was headed for the library
which flanked the temple.

The most striking demonstration of the potential power of this form
of speech is the desperate risk which Lucretius runs in order to combat it,
when he opens his philosophical poem with what must have been at the
time the most beautiful and magnificent hymn ever written in the language.[109] We have already glanced at the opening of *De rerum natura*,
noting how Lucretius's first line alludes to three prestigious ways of
troping the goddess Venus, as a figure of politics, myth, or philosophy

---

[107] Selden (1992), on the deliberate absence of a context for 49 (*disertissime Romuli nepotum*) or 8 (*miser Catulle*).   [108] Williams (1968), 155.

[109] An Ariadne's thread in Gale (1994), 208–23.

(p. 16). His invocation of Venus as Muse, generative principle, and guarantor of imperial peace is a shock to the reader's casual knowledge about Epicureanism, for if anyone knew anything about Epicurean philosophy it was that the gods did not intervene in mundane affairs. Lucretius is not a victim of the discourses he emblematically juxtaposes in his first line, however, but master of the fertile energy that comes from their collocation. By the end of the poem the ideal reader may be in a position to see how this stunning overture is Lucretius' most daring example of '*unmasking*, in which we are first presented with a familiar image or *façon de parler* and then shocked into an awareness that it conceals a piece of Epicurean truth'.[110] The hymn becomes another way of catching *horror ac diuina uoluptas*, the intoxication and awe which is for Lucretius the hallmark of genuine philosophical revelation. In the proem to Book 3 he describes that sensation 'directly', as a response to the reading of Epicurus (14–30). On re-reading the poem, we see that this intoxication has already been presented to us in the very first lines, in terms which had then appeared familiar, but which at this stage require complete reassessment, for now we know that pleasure and peace are the philosophical goods of Epicurus, and that our true 'ally' is not Venus (*sociam*, 1.24), but Ἐπίκουρος, 'Epicurus', himself one to be regarded as a god (5.8).[111] The *uoluptas* which is truly *diuina* is not the property of the Roman Venus but of the Greek Epicurus.

The hymnic language has not become a husk, however, for the sublimity of the Epicurean religious vision has been sporadically revealed to us over the course of the poem. If we had slackly thought that Epicureans were atheists, the poem has confounded us; and our first rereading of the opening will re-educate us into seeing that only Epicureans are truly religious, truly capable of using such language aright. If such language had had no power in Rome of the late Republic, Lucretius' audacity would have been vacuous.

Genres of belief in contest

Lucretius is an advocate of a totalising philosophical discourse, but even he cannot cut away from the non-philosophical, and necessarily remains

[110] Hardie (1986), 236; cf. Clay (1983), 49 for this process, and Gale (1994), 212–14 on the 'redefining' and 'fragmenting' of Venus as the poem goes on.
[111] Gale (1994), 137, on the translingual pun (ἐπίκουρος is 'ally' in Greek).

in dialogue with it while championing his philosophy's claim to sole truth. For those writers who are not advocating the tenets of a school, there is no master-discourse at all, no bedrock of core belief to be recovered after removing the overlay. This does not mean that the issue of belief is inert or of no relevance, as the modern comparative studies of religion may sometimes appear to imply. Rather, the issue of belief is potentially once again in play in each piece of writing. The problems of belief are addressed from the beginnings of ancient literary criticism, and they find expression in what we may call 'religious' contexts, even if the terms of debate are not the same as in a Christian context.[112]

Seneca, for example, deploys the language of belief to devastating effect in his *Apocolocyntosis*, when he depicts the deified Augustus speaking in a council of the gods against the motion to deify Claudius. 'Who will worship *this* person as a god?', says Augustus at the climax of his speech, 'Who will believe that he is a god? So long as you make gods like this, no one will believe that *you* are gods' (*hunc deum quis colet? quis credet? dum tales deos facitis, nemo uos deos esse credet, Apoc.* 11.4). In this narrative, the question of what kind of belief or observance we give the dead emperor Claudius gains extra bite from the self-referential challenge to our ideas about the various kinds of belief we have in the dead emperor Augustus. After all, we have at least two 'beliefs' in our heads about Augustus as we read the *Apocolocyntosis*. Augustus is at first a believable figure in the fiction, an entirely plausible player in a fictional world of divine councils which, ever since the *Aeneid* and the *Metamorphoses*, had come increasingly to be modelled on his own senatorial management (as Seneca acknowledges with a splendid joke in chapter 9, when Diespiter caps his motion in favour of Claudius' apotheosis with the recommendation that his jargon be added as a footnote to Ovid's *Metamorphoses*). With his rhetorical questions, however, Augustus reminds his readers that they also have another kind of 'belief' in him, as the object of state cult.

Seneca uses such language of cult in the *De Clementia*, where he remarks that 'it is not because we are ordered to that we believe Augustus is a god' (*deum esse non tamquam iussi credimus*, 1.10.3). In the *De Clementia*, *credere* is not part of a personal credo, but a reference to the 'observance' of the cult, and part of a protreptic argument designed to

---

[112] See n.30 above.

make the young Nero act in such a way as to deserve such cult himself. In the *Apocolocyntosis*, this same language of cult observance is startlingly undermined by the reminder that our primary belief in Augustus at this point is as a player in Seneca's fantasy. The discrepancy between what we believe as readers of the fiction and what we believe as participants in state cult is sharpened by the fact that the outcome of the fiction is not the same as the outcome of reality. In the story, Claudius' bid for apotheosis is defeated, but in reality he was deified, the first Roman emperor to join the ranks of the gods since the nonpareil, Augustus, exactly forty years earlier.

The problem of belief can always be made to matter. When such language is used, however, it is not relating to a constant kernel of agreed and revealed belief, but is part of an ongoing contestation between different forms of speech over whether and how any particular application is going to be made to stick. The criteria of truth and belief remain variable because they are radically contextual, being always produced from ever-changing conditions of dialogue. The interaction between myth and philosophy in the second half of the first century BCE is a striking example of this process, as we observe different discourses jostling for position against each other, producing new conditions for meaning in the process. Momigliano sees a shift from the Ciceronian and Caesarian age to the Augustan age, in which 'poetry replaces philosophy in the discussion about religion',[113] and one can see why he talks in these terms. Lucretius' Epicurean cosmic de-mythologising is combated by Virgil's imperial re-mythologising, and in Ovid's *Metamorphoses* this process is carried on even further, so that the authority of philosophy dwindles to the point of becoming just another voice.[114] The *Aeneid* strikingly exemplifies the power of poetic mythology in the new era. We have already noted Horace's affirmation of the *Aeneid* as a new frame for Roman experience within two years of its author's death (p. 36), and recent studies have traced the way in which the poem, with its national myth, made its way into the heart of the régime's religious programme.[115]

By begging the question of the power of myth in Roman culture, however, we have run ahead of the argument. It is time to turn to 'Myth'.

---

[113] Momigliano (1987), 62; cf. Liebeschuetz (1979), 89.

[114] Hardie (1986), on Lucretius and Virgil; Solodow (1988), 162–8, and Myers (1994), 54–7, 132, on Ovid.

[115] Graf (1988), 68; Zanker (1988), 193–210; Scheid (1993).

CHAPTER

2

Myth

An old antithesis

The topic of 'myth' is filled with preconceptions about Roman and Greek literature and culture which have been assimilated to some degree by every classicist, and which remain highly recalcitrant to unearthing. We have already discussed the invidious way in which scholars generally frame comparisons between Greek and Roman literature and religion, but in myth more than any other cultural sphere the primacy and energy of the Greeks' activity appears automatically to weaken any Roman counterpart. 'Myth' simply is '*Greek* myth', not only to contemporary classicists but to the first students of comparative religion in the early nineteenth century and for at least a century afterwards.[1] Myth at Rome is consequently often seen as derivative and parasitic, a borrowing from a more creative foreign culture in order to make up for something naturally missing: 'The Greeks were far more advanced and original than the Romans, supplying them from very early times with many of the myths and ideas about their own gods.'[2]

The resulting frame of mind is instinctively hostile to Roman mythopoesis. When Bruit Zaidman and Schmitt Pantel discuss Pausanias' account of Mantinea's cults, for example, they mention Aphrodite Melainis in respectful terms, before turning to Aphrodite's cult at the foot of Mt. Anchisia: this cult they describe as 'lié à la légende récente, colportée par les Romains, de son union avec Anchise, père

---

[1] Phillips (1991a), 143, 149; Graf (1993a), esp. 32, 34, 43.
[2] Ogilvie (1981), 4.

47

d'Enée'. In the English translation Cartledge suppresses 'récente', no
doubt remembering that this tale goes back almost a thousand years to
the age of Homer, and that it had featured in Roman ideology for at least
400 years by Pausanias' time; but the general sardonic tone is well
preserved – 'associated with the legend, peddled by the Romans, of
Venus' union with Ankhises (father of Aeneas)'.[3] Revealingly, the most
damning aspect of this dismissal is the choice of word to describe the
ancient tale: as soon as Rome is under discussion, we are presented not
with 'myth', but 'legend'.

According to the Greek model, myth is a traditionally hallowed,
communally significant cultural phenomenon, and these terms throw
into relief the apparently self-evident contrast with Rome, where the lack
of a native equivalent has long been a scandal: in the words of Mary
Beard, 'it is the comparison with Greek culture that is central to the
whole "problem" of Roman myth and myth-making – its absence from,
or marginality to, the central arenas of Roman culture'.[4] Already in the
ancient world there were those who remarked upon the supposed lack of
Roman myth, although their priorities were very different from those of
modern scholars, for the ancient observers saw this lack in a positive, not
a negative light.[5] The stories Dionysius of Halicarnassus missed in the
Roman tradition were the cosmogonic myths of divine castration and
infanticide, together with tales of rape, war, and slavery (*Ant. Rom.*
2.19.1–2).[6] These myths had attracted philosophical censure in Greece
since the sixth century, and it was therefore held to the Romans' credit
that they did not have this stock of outrageous tales; paradoxically – at
least to modern eyes – it was precisely their high opinion of Roman piety
that led both Greek and Roman intellectuals to stress and praise the
Roman lack of such myths.[7]

The apparent lack of a native Roman equivalent to Greek mythopoesis has spurred many modern scholars into 'looking (harder) for Roman myth' (in the phrase of Beard (1993)). 'Historical' or 'historicising'

---

[3] Bruit Zaidman and Schmitt Pantel (1992), 213.
[4] Beard (1993), 47. I must declare here the general debt which the present chapter owes
to this powerful paper.
[5] Cic. *Nat. D.* 3.60; Dion. Hal. *Ant. Rom.* 2.18–20, with Gabba (1991), 118–38 and
Bourgeaud (1993).   [6] Important discussion by Price in BNP, Vol. 1, Ch. 4.
[7] The phenomenon which struck Dionysius was therefore quite circumscribed, relating to a particular category of myth: Bourgeaud (1993), 176–7.

myth has long been a popular area in which to search for quintessentially Roman mythic activity, and more recently Wiseman has argued for an ancient indigenous Roman mythic tradition, based on dramatic festivals and oral story-telling.[8] There are many gains to be made in these areas of research, but there are also many problems. Chief among them is the often unspoken assumption that the only authentic Roman or Italian mythic activity is the indigenous and original. Inevitably, such an assumption distracts attention from the fact that the great mass of the mythological material in the surviving remains of Roman culture is Greek. Nicholas Horsfall, for example, well documents the enthusiasm with which 'popular culture embraced imported myth',[9] yet persists in regarding only 'native myths' as his legitimate quarry in a book entitled *Roman Myth and Mythography*. Oddly enough, in view of her usual insistence that the study of Roman religion should concentrate on the central body of historical evidence instead of on such marginal spheres as origins or mystery cults, even Beard falls prey to the urge to locate Roman mythic activity somewhere other than in an engagement with the Greek mythology that dominates our Roman evidence.[10]

The fact is that from the beginning of Roman literature Greek mythology is everywhere, in vast bulk, and an account of mythology in Rome which is going to be of any use to students of the literature must concentrate on the Greek dimension. We must do this, however, in the face of the stubbornly rooted notion that there is a hole in Roman culture where genuine myth ought to be, and that Greek myth is a mere supplement to a native Roman lack. It is precisely when we come to study Greek myth in Rome that Roman mythic activity appears to be most obviously derivative and inauthentic, not only because it seems not to be a 'native' or 'indigenous' activity, but also because the comparison throws into high relief the traditionally accepted contrast with the primary and socially grounded mythopoesis of Greece.

---

[8] See Beard (1993), 44–50, for an overview and critique of the views of Georges Dumézil, Grant (1971) and Wiseman (1989) – add now Wiseman (1995) and Fox (1996).   [9] Bremmer and Horsfall (1987), 4.

[10] Her focus on the declamation schools in Beard (1993) is a rhetorical move, of course, designed to force a reassessment of how we regard the problem of myth, but it still leaves untouched (with the exception of 50 n.15) the problem of how to read the central body of evidence. See now, however, Beard (1996), for a direct engagement with the problem of Greek myth in Rome.

The prevalent antithesis between mythic activity in Greece and Rome is formulated by Horsfall with deliberately provocative trenchancy in words whose pithiness has already proved irresistible for quotation to others:

> The poets of classical Greece create or retell myth for society at large; Roman men of letters construct secondary myth for *recitationes*. In that context it exercises little or no 'social function'.[11]

The antitheses are stark. The most potent of all has its other half unspoken, for 'secondary' is left hanging, with 'primary' unexpressed. If 'primary' had been expressed it would have opened up one of the biggest cracks in this antithetical construction: a poet can 'retell' primary myth, but how can he 'create' it? If it is 'primary' it is already there.

Such antitheses perpetuate an impossibly Romantic view of Greek culture, which paralyses at the outset any attempt to study myth in Rome or any other literate culture. Building on the conclusions of the first chapter, I shall make the case for a more dynamic model of cultural interchange between Rome and Greece, one that will allow us to see that such trans-cultural contact may be an enrichment, rather than a diminution, of a society's imaginative and intellectual resources. I shall argue that, far from being 'secondary' or 'derivative', the Roman engagement with Greek myth was radically innovative and creative, forging a trans-cultural sensibility with which we are still living. Shelley may have said 'We are all Greeks', but in this regard we are all Romans.

Never pre-Greek

We need first to register the pervasiveness of Greek myth in Roman life. Language of 'lack', 'secondary', 'inauthentic' can obscure the density and antiquity of Greek myth in Rome, and its important role in the life of the state.[12] The ubiquity of Greek elements in the life and cult of regal and early Republican Rome was already remarked upon in the first chapter (pp. 26–7), and acquaintance with Greek myth was likewise part of this same cultural exchange. Like other towns in Latium and central Italy, early Rome was host to Etruscan and Greek artists and traders

---

[11] Bremmer and Horsfall (1987), 1; his quoted phrase refers to the argument of Burkert (1979), 2.   [12] Wiseman (1995), esp. 35–42.

who produced and imported diverse representations of Greek myth. Even before the establishment of the Republic, we have a Minotaur depicted on a terracotta fragment from the Regia, and, in the form of a terracotta statue group from the S. Ombono sanctuary in the Forum Boarium, a representation of Athena introducing Heracles to Olympus (c. 530 BCE).[13] The pairing of Athena and Heracles is a particularly striking case, for it is very probably an element of monarchical ideology, reflecting contemporary Greek tyrannical propaganda.[14] From the beginning, then, Greek myth may be part of public ideology at Rome, drawing its power from far beyond the state's boundaries.

In the case of Athena in the Forum Boarium, it is a question whether we should actually say 'Minerva'. It certainly seems as if the practice of finding such analogies was already underway even this early. Coarelli's excavation of what he identifies as Vulcan's shrine in the Forum produced an Attic pot showing Hephaestus' return to Olympus; the obvious implication is that someone – Greek, Roman, or Etruscan – was making some kind of identification between Vulcan and Hephaestus even in the 580s or 570s BCE, 350 years before Roman literature began.[15]

We cannot know how naturalised such Greek myths were in early Rome. The Romans, however, as we saw in Chapter 1, were always very careful to refrain from full domestication of Greek cult in their city, sustaining instead a dialogue between native and imported cults; and we shall see below that in the historical period it was likewise important for them to be able to maintain an awareness that Greek myth was ultimately from somewhere else.[16] It is possible that a sense of difference and distance, however faint and variable, was an important element of the cultural work Greek myth was doing at Rome from the start.

The presence of Greek mythic representations at Rome may be ancient, but the importance of periodisation is immediately apparent, for there are two definite principal phases in Roman receptiveness to Greek cult, and – so we may probably assume by analogy – to Greek culture generally. In terms of cult, we may mark the end of the first phase with the introduction of Apollo in 431 BCE– the last import of the early Republic. After that, a hiatus of 130 years, until the explosion of hellenising adaptation and innovation which began around 300 (signalled

[13] Boardman (1994), 272–9; Wiseman (1995), 37–9; Cornell (1995), 147–8.
[14] Cornell (1995), 148.   [15] Coarelli (1983), 177; cf. Cornell (1995), 162–3.
[16] Above, pp. 26–7; below, pp. 64–7.

especially by the introduction of the cult of Aesculapius in 291), and
which continued down to the end of the Hannibalic War, with the
importation of Magna Mater in 204.[17] These two broad periods of
receptivity to hellenisation in cult show a rough overlap with Wiseman's
more general periodisation, by which 'Rome can be described as "Hel-
lenized" in the archaic and Hellenistic periods of Greek culture, . . . and
not in the classical period'.[18]

The first Greeks to write literature in Latin

Whether, or how, mythic narratives – Greek or 'native' – might have
survived in Rome over the 'dark age', as Wiseman calls it, is a question
which will no doubt continue to be debated. For us, as students of the
surviving literature, the point may fairly be held to be moot, for the
beginning of Roman literature is very firmly in the middle of the second
of these two main hellenising periods, when the city, already well stocked
for centuries with Greek cult and representations of Greek myth, had
been launched for half a century on a new period of hellenising experimentation. And the literary men who played their part in this process
during the first generations were, of course, themselves Greek or 'half-
Greek' (*semigraeci*, Suet. *Gram.* 1).[19] These men, such as the Greek from
Tarentum, Andronikos, who became Livius, a *ciuis Romanus*, inhabited
volatile interstices between Greek and Roman culture. Or else, more
commonly, they inhabited the interstices between *three* linguistic cultures, with Greek and Latin as numbers two and three, and the first
being Oscan (Naevius), Oscan or Messapian (Ennius), Umbrian
(Plautus), Celtic (Statius Caecilius), or Punic (Terence).[20] So interstitial
an activity is the writing of this new literature, indeed, that it appears to
be seventy years before anyone participates who is a Roman citizen and
a Latin speaker by birth (Cato the Censor); when Romans turned their
hand to 'literature' in these first generations, they wrote history, and they
wrote it not in Latin but in Greek.[21]

---

[17] Garnsey and Saller (1987), 170; on the early third century in particular, see Weinstock (1957).   [18] Wiseman (1989), 132; cf. Cornell (1995), 397.

[19] An introductory sketch in Feeney (1991), 100–2.

[20] Jocelyn (1972), 991; Momigliano (1975), 17; Bakhtin (1981), 63.

[21] Badian (1966), 6–7, on Q. Fabius Pictor, L. Cincius Alimentus, C. Acilius, and A.
Postumius Albinus.

In creating a national literature in the vernacular on the model of another national literature, these denizens of the overlapping cultures of central and southern Italy were engaged in an undertaking which no one in the Mediterranean had ever contemplated before, but which became a paradigm for later literary history.[22] The invention of Roman literature is one of the most extraordinary events in history, yet we tend to regard it as inevitable, just a matter of time. In fact, the question to ask is not why it happened quite when it did, but why it happened at all.

We shall return to these observations on the first creators of Roman literature at the end of the chapter. For now, we need only remark that the new Roman literature was from the beginning shot through with its inventors' Greek literature and scholarship, with all their mythological freight. With unflagging zest the first poets of Latin literature embraced every conceivable variety of mythological and religious discourse. Ennius is the most spectacular example: translator of Euhemerus and Epicharmus, and creator of a Roman national epic which included pontifical ritual, Pythagoreanism, Homeric anthropomorphic deities, euhemerism, and much else.[23] All of this self-conscious, exuberant intellectual diversity is taking place in a city which, as we have seen, is full of Greek cult and representations of Greek myth, and is by this time long habituated to the principal names and events of the pan-Hellenic mythic cycle.[24] By the second century BCE even quite recherché Greek myths appear on Roman coinage, minted by aristocrats anxious to link their families with the glamour and prestige of the heroic and divine world, addressing a receptive and knowledgeable general audience.[25] As a great Hellenistic city, Rome is adept at the contemporary Greek techniques of configuring civic ideology in mythic terms.[26]

As an example of how Greek myth could be keyed in to vital concerns of the Roman state, and of how the resulting complex could be figured in Roman literature, let us briefly consider two cases: the Gigantomachy, and the demi-god Hercules.

---

[22] Fantham (1989), 220. Cf. Jocelyn (1972), 991: 'The Sabellians, Umbrians and Messapians had been heavily influenced by Greek culture but although they used their respective languages in the Greek way for religious and legal purposes there is no evidence that they ever acquired a written literature.' The Romans were in precisely this position before 240 BCE. See Horsfall (1994) for the pre-literary forms of Roman society.   [23] Feeney (1991), 120–8.

[24] A masterly exposition in Fraenkel (1960), Ch. 3, 'Elementi mitologici', esp. 85–7.

[25] Wiseman (1974).   [26] Barchiesi (1962), 227.

Greek myths in the service of the Roman state

In the burst of religious and cultic innovation in the early third century, the brothers Cn. and Q. Ogulnius stand out as conspicuous reformers. As tribunes of the plebs in 300 BCE, they were responsible for opening up the colleges of *augures* and *pontifices* to plebeians (Liv. 10.6.4–6), and in 292 Quintus led the delegation to Epidaurus which invited the healing god to migrate to Rome as Aesculapius (Val. Max. 1.8.2). In 296, as the Romans prepared for the climactic encounter with the Celtic-Samnite coalition, the brothers were curule aediles, and they erected two pieces of bronze statuary, whose different themes offer an object lesson in the Romans' self-consciousness about Roman and Greek compartmentalisation. One statue depicted the (perhaps newly authoritative) Roman foundation-myth, the wolf suckling Romulus and Remus, and it was placed near the *ficus Ruminalis*, where the wolf supposedly found the exposed twins;[27] the other represented Jupiter in his four-horse chariot, brandishing the thunder-bolt, and it was placed on the temple of Jupiter Optimus Maximus (Liv. 10.23.12). Jupiter's pose was that of Zeus in triumph over the offspring of Earth, playing his role in the Gigantomachy, a Greek myth now being taken over by the Romans – itself, of course, a myth taken over by the Greeks from Near Eastern stories of the Weather-God's defeat of monsters who threaten his reign.[28]

Towards the end of the third century, the poet Naevius wrote the first poem on Roman history, taking the First Punic War as his subject. In the first book he described a Gigantomachy on some artefact or other (fr. 8 Büchner). We do not know what function this paradigm was discharging in his poem.[29] Certainly, since his audience had been living with a Gigantomachic Jupiter in the city for almost a century, it seems misguided to assume that they would have responded to a Gigantomachy in an historical poem as being 'artificial', 'Greek', 'literary' – to itemise only the chief of the disparaging terms which Latinists have applied to Greek myth in Roman literary texts. We have to beware, however, of assuming that the case snaps shut because our text appears to have reference to a civic cultic paradigm which is familiar to the audience. We are not necessarily solving the interpretative problem at a stroke by asserting

---

[27] Wiseman (1995), 72–6 for speculation.   [28] Vian (1952), 285–6.
[29] For speculation, see Feeney (1991), 118–19; Goldberg (1995), 52.

that our text is referring to something solidly and reassuringly naturalised as Roman. Rather, the text is engaged in a circuit of meaning that is
formed by the currents of high Greco-Roman culture, in which self-
conscious compartmentalising is always potentially at issue. The Greekness of that cult image was highly marked when it was commissioned in
tandem with the Romulean wolf, and I regard it as very probable that
the Greekness of the Gigantomachic paradigm was now revivified and
accentuated by Naevius for paradoxical purposes: the Romans are
taking over from the Greeks, inserting themselves into the ancient Greek
military and cultural role of defenders of civilization against the barbarian.[30] If this is right, then the power of the Romans' insertion into the
paradigm depended precisely upon the audience's capacity to refuse
simply to co-opt Greek imagery so that it became internalised as naturally Roman.

Our second case of Greek myth in a publicly charged context is that of
the demi-god Hercules, and it takes us down to the Augustan age. We
may read the eighth book of Virgil's *Aeneid*, with its obsessive interest in
Hercules, as an intelligent – if rather recherché – redeployment of Greek
categories of god, demi-god, and human: the poet can focus on the
hazards of stupendous mortal achievement with the aid of a structuralist
schema drawn from his foreign literary sources. But for at least 150 years
before Virgil was born, and possibly much longer, his fellow-citizens had
been viewing processions before the games, the *pompa circensis*, in which
divine images were, very probably, grouped according to just these
divisions: first the twelve Olympian gods – itself a Greek category – and
then Hercules, Castor and Pollux, Aesculapius, the sons of gods by
mortal mothers.[31] These mythic categorisations were part of the state's
religious apparatus, and therefore part of the mental equipment of
Virgil's readers.

While such categories may have been part of civic ritual for centuries,
they take on a completely new life in this era, mutating rapidly under the
pressures of new ideologies – witness Caesar's insertion of his own image

---

[30] Feeney (1991), 119.

[31] On the *pompa circensis*, see Latte (1960), 248–50; Long (1987), 239–42. Long rightly
stresses that it is not certain that the twelve gods were allotted their own category in
the procession; Roman cult had, however, grouped the Twelve in other contexts for
two centuries by Virgil's time (Long, 236–7), and it seems likely that they maintained the category in the *pompa*.

beside that of Victoria in the *pompa* before the *Ludi Victoriae Caesaris* in
July 45 BCE (Cic. *Att.* 336.1). The point about Hercules in Virgil's *Aeneid*
is that he escapes human categories and inserts himself into divine ones,
as Aeneas had done, as Julius Caesar had done, and as Caesar's son,
Augustus, was himself doing at the time that the *Aeneid* was being
written. Horace's *C.* 1.12 is the most schematic exposition of the di-
lemma of how to categorise Augustus: 'Which man or demi-god do you
sing', he asks the Muse, 'which god?' (*quem uirum aut heroa . . . quem
deum?*, 1–3). By the end of the poem the problem has become one of
deciding whether Augustus belongs in one, two, or three of these categories. As Simon Price has shown, this is a question people all over the
world were trying to answer.[32]

And all the 'other' Greek myths?

Greek myths and mythic paradigms, then, could be a vital part of
Roman public life, and a vital part of literature about that public life.
This is nowadays a comparatively uncontroversial position, at least in
discussions of the Augustan age, where the mythological dimensions of
the régime's ritual and cultural programme have recently received numerous excellent treatments.[33] But what are we to say of Greek myth at
Rome in contexts which are not obviously interacting with the public
realm in the ways we have been examining? The status of Augustus
means something in Roman society, and the mythic paradigms constructed by and around Augustus mean something in Roman society. But
Ovid's afflicted damsels turning into bears and trees and birds, this surely
is just Greek, a literary exercise, not something integral to the culture but
something foreign to be 'used' or 'exploited' or 'drawn upon'.[34] Here the
supposed artificiality or inauthenticity of the Roman product is most
overt.

Virgil may remould the myth of the Golden and Iron Ages to create
his picture of nature and civilization in the *Georgics*. Ovid may deploy
the entire range of Greek myth to create his vision of the limits and
possibilities of human experience in the *Metamorphoses*. And these
treatments of myth may resonate for two millennia afterwards. Yet

---

[32] Price (1984). We return to *C.* 1.12 below (pp. 111–13).
[33] Hardie (1986); Zanker (1988); Hölscher (1993); Scheid (1993).
[34] Cf. Beard (1993), 45–6.

students of Roman culture continue to be reluctant to ascribe vitality to Roman mythopoesis. Students of post-Classical European cultures, indeed, habituated to the domination of Roman mythic paradigms in their own areas of speciality, may regard the cultural power of Virgilian or Ovidian or Senecan myth as self-evident, and may wonder at the expense of effort in proving it. Such a starting-point is not as natural for professional Latinists, however, who are looking back over their shoulders at Alcaeus and Pindar rather than forwards to Dante and Shakespeare and Freud. The working assumption amongst the community of Latinists continues to be that the Roman writers are engaged in a qualitatively different exercise from their Greek counterparts (not, be it noted, from their Greek *contemporaries*, but their counterparts in pre-Hellenistic Greece, with whom, significantly, they are instinctively compared). There are distinctions to be made here, but they are harder to define than most scholars appear to think. In particular, the conventional antitheses are not helpful.

The limits of antithesis

(i) *'Primary' versus 'secondary'*

The distinction between 'primary' myth in Greece and 'secondary' myth in Rome, latent in the antithetical sentence of Horsfall quoted earlier (p. 50), is one most Latinists take for granted. Yet the distinction between primary and secondary myth has been called into question by most recent writers on myth.[35] A theory of myth that is concerned with origins will see its task as somehow authenticating a myth by tracing it back to its pure well-springs. But this search for authentication is inevitably at the expense of looking at what the myth is actually doing, how it works at any given moment of analysis. Such a priority fundamentally misidentifies the place where meaning is to be sought: in the terms of Versnel's aphorism, *'origin* is not to be identified with *meaning'*.[36] Rather, as Jonathan Z. Smith puts it in the course of an attack on the Romantic

[35] Barchiesi (1962), 440–1 already protests eloquently against the disastrous consequences of imposing this polarity on early Roman literature.

[36] Versnel (1993), 242 (his italics), a leading theme of the book (taking in ritual as well); cf. 190, 218, 231, 233; Burkert (1993), 19–20. We return to these issues of origin in Ch. 4, 'Ritual'.

distinction between 'the primal moment of myth and its secondary application': 'there is no pristine myth; there is only application'.[37]

It is striking that scholars seldom talk about any other aspect of culture in these terms of 'primary' and 'secondary', 'original' and 'inauthentic'. The tomato was not used for cooking in Italy until 1700: is the cuisine of contemporary Italy inauthentic? It was only around the same time (to take an example of influence in the reverse direction across the Atlantic) that the Plains Indians of North America started riding horses. The whole nomadic culture of war and hunting, based on the horse, lasted less than two hundred years. It is the quintessential North American Indian culture in the popular imagination, yet only five generations experienced it out of the five hundred to nine hundred generations since the crossing of the Bering Straits. Was the Plains Indians' horse culture then an inauthentic culture? When did the horse stop being an inauthentic part of Comanche or Sioux culture and become an authentic one? In 1750? 1780? 1782? August 1782?

Attuned to the deficiencies of the 'primary/secondary' view of myth and culture, many students of Greek myth are open to the possibility that a myth can be viewed as a myth even if it is not 'immemorially old' and 'indigenous'.[38] Of course, the main reason why they are sympathetic to this position is that they are aware of the fact that a great deal of Greek myth is itself demonstrably not 'immemorially old' and 'indigenous', and cannot 'be assumed to have arisen spontaneously from uncontaminated "origins"; it arose within a society that formed itself in intense competition with older, Eastern civilisations'.[39] Core elements of panhellenic mythology – from the divine succession myths to the Seven against Thebes – may have come from the East into the Greek tradition only shortly before our documentation begins.[40] Indeed, even this conventional way of framing the issue may not do justice to the aleatory nature of much of this process. It has been argued that such apparently fundamental myths as the Trojan Horse, or the Judgement of Paris, or Heracles and the Hydra arose as late as the eighth century, as the result of attempts to explain Greek artists' representations of a Near Eastern

[37] Smith (1978), 299; cf. 206, 308; Smith (1982), 88–9; and his contribution in Hamerton-Kelly (1987), arguing the same case for ritual (esp. 195). For similar points in the context of Greek myth, see Parker (1987), 188; Brillante (1990), 114–15.
[38] Graf (1993a), 36 ('uralt', 'indigen').   [39] Burkert (1987), 11.
[40] Burkert (1993), 20; in general, West (1988); Burkert (1992).

iconography which they did not understand: 'some pictures we take to be illustrations of Greek myths must have given rise to Greek myths'.[41]

No one to my knowledge impugns the 'authenticity' of Greek myth on this count (though, as we shall see, it can cause Hellenists some anxieties when they are dealing with the supposedly communal nature of myth). Further, the observable mutability of Greek myth in historical times, especially as part of an ongoing political 'invention of tradition', is often mentioned as one of its most distinctive features, without these new or drastically altered myths being marked down as less 'original' and more 'secondary'. Myths were ceaselessly being redevised and invented for all kinds of reasons. The Athenian invention of the Theseus myth from the end of the sixth century is a clear example.[42] Again, the myth of a battle between the Athenians and Amazons is 'not attested earlier than the Persian Wars',[43] yet it would be passing strange to censure the myth's presence on the Stoa Poikile or Parthenon as inauthentic. 'Non-political' myths, likewise, are open to radical redefinition.[44] Two features would appear to be essential to the core of the Medea myth, for example: she is a barbarian, and she kills her children. Yet it is possible that both of these motifs were invented by Euripides for his play of 431 BCE.[45] What does the Medea myth look like in 432? In sum, many would agree with Bremmer's contention that 'it is precisely this improvisatory character of myth that guarantees its centrality in Greek religion'.[46]

Roman inventiveness and secondariness, however, is regarded very differently from Greek. Horsfall, for example, has written illuminatingly on the malleability of myth in the Greek archaic and classical literary tradition;[47] his readiness to see mythic invention as culturally dynamic in Greece highlights his unwillingness to see it as dynamic in Rome. The capacity of myth to be invented or taken over from other cultures is brought forward as proof of the vitality of the Greek system and of the artificiality of the Roman.

I am not claiming that processes of cultural interaction are constant, so that the Romans simply did to the Greeks what the Greeks had earlier

[41] Powell (1997); cf. Morris (1992), 116, 163, 184.
[42] Parker (1987); Morris (1992), 336–57; Graf (1993b), 136–40; Calame (1995), 189–201.   [43] Morris (1992), 312.   [44] March (1987).
[45] Hall (1992), 194–5.
[46] Bremmer (1987), 3–4 (though I would change the last word to 'culture').
[47] Horsfall (1993), 135–7.

done to their own Eastern neighbours. Later in the chapter we shall
discuss the nature of the differences in more detail. At this stage my aim
is more limited, merely to make the basic point that we will be throwing
out a lot of Greek myth as well as Roman if our criteria for selection are
whether or not a myth came from somewhere else, or whether or not a
myth was invented or fundamentally redesigned.

(ii) *The collectivist Golden Age of Greece versus the Iron Age of Rome*

The criterion of 'belief' will not help, either, if it is claimed that the
difference between myth in Greece and myth in Rome is that the Greeks
believed in their myths and the Romans did not.[48] With the help of
Veyne, I have already tried to put some pressure on this question of what
is involved in claiming that the Greeks did 'believe in their myths', and
we need not retrace our steps in detail.[49] It goes without saying that the
Romans inherited attitudes to myth and fiction which had been crystal-
lised well after the classical period, and that the problems of belief facing
them were not the same as the problems of belief facing audiences and
composers in archaic and classical Greece. Still, that there were problems of belief in archaic and classical Greece seems impossible to deny, if
only because, as any anthropologist knows, 'belief-nonbelief is an active
problem in any community where legends are told'.[50]

Such a perspective is not popular among students of early Greece,
however, because it offends against the collectivist and oral model which
underpins their view of myth. Hence another of the antitheses marked
out by Horsfall: in Greece, the audience for myth is 'society at large',
while in Rome it is *'recitationes'*, and 'in that context [myth] exercises
little or no "social function"'.[51] The danger here is that we fall prey to a
Romanticising view of Greek society, as a Golden Age where audience
and poet are at one in a matrix of communal meaning, with agency

---

[48] Note the untypically blunt formulation of Graf (1993a), 29: 'Zuzugeben ist, dass in
Rom Mythos als Fiktion galt, während er in der homerischen oder sophokleischen
Dichtererzählung geglaubte Vergangenheit war'; the footnote to this sentence,
referring to Veyne (1988), sits like a depth charge at the bottom of the page.

[49] pp. 22–5; I refer once more to the important work of Bowie (1993) and Pratt
(1993).   [50] Dégh and Vázsonyi (1976), 109.

[51] Bremmer and Horsfall (1987), 1.

effaced ('the polis representing itself to itself'). It is interesting to observe how far back this Golden Age has to be pushed for the idealised model of the communal mythic system to work: '[Myth's] function is most vital in closed archaic societies', according to Burkert;[52] and the onset of the post-Golden Iron Age is accordingly located already in the sixth century or in classical Athens by many scholars.[53]

Still, distinctions between different periods of Greek culture tend to be effaced when the focus is on the difference between Greece and Rome, for Hellenists and Latinists alike draw comparisons between the complex, pluralistic, hot society of Rome and the simpler, closed, communal, cold society of the early Greek *polis*, where everyone shares the same oral tradition.[54] Yet the larger sociological assumptions behind this opposition seem fundamentally misconceived, and are regarded with increasing scepticism by many contemporary anthropologists, who concentrate instead on the volatility which even the most 'primitive' cultures exhibit both internally and in their interactions with other cultures:

> Stark 'great divide' contrasts between 'modern' and 'pre-modern' societies, the one individualistic, rational, and free of tradition, the other collectivistic, intuitive, and mired in it, look increasingly mythical, summary, and simple-minded.[55]

Smith makes the point with characteristic vigour:

> There's an enormous anachronism to the notion of the collective . . . Pluralism is as old as mankind . . . The diversity and pluralism of any so-called primitive society can be found to be as complicated as modern San Francisco.[56]

After all, where and when in Greece is this idealised primary and communal state to be found? In democratic Athens? The first imperial

---

[52] Burkert (1987), 11; cf. Graf (1992), 22 and (1993a), 43; Bremmer (1987), 4–5.

[53] Sixth century: Woodbury (1985), 206; classical Athens: Herington (1985), 63–4; Hölscher (1993), 71.

[54] The strong influence of symbolic anthropology on Greek studies is evident here: see Desan (1989), 64–5 for a critique of symbolic anthropology's definition of culture 'primarily as a collectively held system of symbols', which 'ultimately stresses culture's role as a kind of subtle mechanism for the maintenance of order, meaning, and social cohesion'; cf. Bloch (1989), 106–36.

[55] Geertz (1994), 3; cf. Bloch (1989), esp. 119–20; and Clifford (1988), 250 n.13, for bibliography.   [56] Smith (1987), 187–8.

power of the West, a communal body of about 40,000 citizens, owning at least 60,000 slaves, running an empire that covered 70,000 square miles of sea and land?[57] In one of the states of archaic Greece? Yet these states are among the most innovative and competitive units the world has seen, riven with civil strife, inventing and reforming constitutions, experimenting with new cultural forms made possible by the revolutionary technology of the alphabet, throwing colonies all over the world from France to the Black Sea, interacting with the cultures of the Near East so as to produce 'innovations in religion, poetry, and politics that manifest themselves in the transformations known as archaic art and culture'.[58] What society at large is being addressed here? Did Homer address society at large? Did Hesiod? Did Ibycus? Sappho?

If we follow Horsfall in claiming that 'society at large' has to be the audience before we allow myth any 'social function', we find ourselves involved in a paring-away argument about how large a percentage of society myth has to reach or elicit a response from before it qualifies as myth: 30%? 15%? 14%? Ideally, one feels, many would like the answer to be as close to 100% as possible, with myth being communally available, learnt from infancy. The mystique of the oral asserts itself strongly at this point. It is by no means clear, however, that myths were part of everyday or popular discourse.[59] Indeed, it is arguable that the dissemination of myth in early Greece was not an exclusively oral phenomenon, but linked also to the dynamic and diffusive power of the new alphabetic technology.[60] The notion that myth is more authentic if it is grounded in the folk is, of course, very specifically Romantic: one may compare the widespread idea that the brothers Grimm recorded their stories from indigenous peasants, despite the clear evidence that their sources were primarily 'educated young women from the middle class or aristocracy', some of them native French-speakers.[61]

---

[57] Cf. Veyne (1988), 45: 'Do we really believe that classical Athens was a great civic collectivity where all minds acted in concert, where the theater ratified the union among hearts, and where the average citizen could pass any test about Jocasta or the return of the Heraclidae?' I am afraid that the answer is very often 'Yes'.

[58] Morris (1992), 148.   [59] Veyne (1988), 43–5; Graf (1993b), 4–5; Powell (1997).

[60] Powell (1997).

[61] Zipes (1987), xxiv–v. Beard (1993), 57–8 has made a cogent case against the use of oralist mystique to deny Roman literary myth any 'social function', arguing that 'it simply cannot be the case that...the story of Tarpeia, for example, is mere literature when in the hands of Propertius, though highly loaded myth when told around some army campfire'.

There were many different social contexts for the reception of myth in archaic and classical Greece, even though many of these contexts are, in effect, irrecoverable. They range from the dozen men at a symposium to the 20,000 people in the audience at the state festivals of Athens. It is fruitless to make all these contexts an amalgam in order to point a contrast with Rome. No literature is without a social context, certainly not in the Roman world, with its libraries and schools, its dissemination of texts over the empire. For the myth in that literature to have a social *function*, however, according to the Hellenic model of myth, it must be referring to 'something of collective importance', in Burkert's words.[62] The communitarian grounding of the Hellenic model at this point immediately comes out into the open once again, for on the basis of this criterion Burkert has explicit reservations about the status of Ovid's *Metamorphoses* as myth: social forms of organisation and practice are what count as 'something of collective importance', not the Ovidian themes of sexuality, mortality and identity.

The limits of the Hellenic model

With the conventional dichotomies found wanting, if we wish to isolate what might be distinctive about myth at Rome we need to begin by offering a more comprehensive objection to the terms in which the debate is conducted. Although I have been expressing reservations about how the Hellenic model of myth is used, especially by Latinists, the argument of the chapter so far has by and large followed the usually tacit assumption that the Hellenic model of myth is *the* model of myth, an assumption that, as we have seen, goes back at least to the early nineteenth century.[63]

This model – primitivist, communal, ritualistic, and preferably oral – is indeed one which even its own advocates can claim to 'work' only for archaic Greece, and we may well wonder what the worth of the hellenocentric model is if not only the Roman Empire and Hellenistic Greece are left out of its purview but even classical Athens. Still, its power is evidently very strong. Any model for the study of myth which puts a high value on origins and ritual or communal grounding will inevitably end up denigrating Roman forms of myth and exalting Greek ones, because it was the Greek forms which such a model was invented to

---

[62] Burkert (1979), 24.   [63] Above, n.1.

explain in the first place. Even on these terms we can 'redeem' much of
the Roman use of Greek myth by giving it its own social or public
ground, as I attempted to show earlier in the chapter, with the examples
of Naevius and Virgil.[64] It is more important, however, to question the
way in which we are using the word 'myth' as a yardstick. For by taking
the word 'myth' over from Greece, we cannot escape from the assumption that the 'myth' of early Greece persists as an identifiable transhistorical category, a phenomenon with certain 'essential' features against
which we may measure the products of any other culture.[65] There are
other possible models of myth, after all, which have served European
culture well for a long time – and many of them the Romans invented.
Let us try turning the prism a few degrees to see how the light falls, to see
whether this may be yet another example, in the long tussle between
these two cultures, of how the Romans turned apparent handicaps into
assets.

A Roman model

Let me recall two earlier points to which I said we would return. First,
the Romans' insistence on maintaining a sense of what was distinctively
Greek in cult and myth in their city. We should remember that this is a
hard cultural choice to make: '*It is far harder to maintain difference than
to overcome it.*'[66] They might, then, have concentrated more on naturalis-
ing and domesticating Greek cult, but, as we have seen, they kept up
elaborate ways of maintaining a sense of difference and distance in this
department of civic life (above, pp. 26–7). They also maintained an
awareness of which myths were Greek, despite their long familiarity with
and assimilation of Greek myth.[67] Their distinctions may well not be the
same ones a modern observer might make, but that is not the point: the
activity of making distinctions is what counts, not their 'accuracy'. By

[64] Cf. Wallace-Hadrill (1982), a path-breaking study in the capacity of myth (the
Myth of Ages) to have a 'social function' in the hands of Virgil, Horace, Ovid and
Augustus.
[65] Calame (1991); Beard (1993), 62; Veyne (1988), 153 n. 210: '"Myth" is not a
transhistorical element or an invariant...Myth is not an essence.' Cf. Graf (1993a), 5,
on the necessity of cutting loose from the Hellenic model in order to make progress in
the study of myth at Rome.   [66] Whitehead (1995), 59 (original emphasis).
[67] Ovid's self-consciousness on this score, for example, emerges very clearly from Graf
(1988); see further below, pp. 69–71 and 126–33.

the time the Romans began their project of a national literature, the Greeks had spent centuries on the task of demarcating myth as a category, and part of the Roman inheritance from Greece was therefore a self-consciousness about the demarcation between the mythic and the non-mythic: in the Romans' culture, the mythic was often to be figured as the 'Greek', so that the process of marking off myth as Greek was an integral part of their hellenisation.

This self-consciousness about the foreign origin of their myths is in marked contrast with the attitudes of the pre-Hellenistic Greeks themselves, who did not maintain an awareness that their cosmogonic myths, for example, had come from somewhere else. Now, it is difficult to make this distinction between the Romans and Greeks without appearing once again to be falsely reducing Greek mythopoesis and cultural interaction to a blander, more primary form. Similarly, we must do justice to the problem of periodisation: the Persian Wars, in particular, were clearly crucial in enforcing a more stark exclusion of the non-Greek.[68] It is entirely possible, for example, that the first audience of Hesiod's *Theogony* were very much aware that they had never heard many of these stories before; it is even possible that Hesiod is playing upon such self-consciousness at the beginning of *Works and Days*, where he gives an indigenous *aition* for human suffering (Pandora) and swiftly follows it with a Near Eastern one (the five Ages, the solitary source of this myth for all later writers).[69] Nonetheless, the important point is that this original awareness – if it existed – did not become part of the poem or its reception. Ready as they were in many contexts and periods to speak of how they took over writing, astrology or divinities from other cultures, the Greeks tended towards the assimilative end of the pole, in comparison with the Romans: 'Transforming imported novelties into native traditions was apparently what Greeks enjoyed and excelled at.'[70] Even the numerous stories about the arrival in Greece of foreign people and cultural practices often turn out to be ultimately ethnocentric;[71] and, crucially, these stories about arrival from abroad do not come marked as being themselves stories that have arrived from abroad. 'Everything that

[68] Hall (1989).
[69] Cf. West (1978), 155 (Pandora a 'traditional myth'); 176–7 (myth of Ages un-Greek); 172 (the two myths incompatible).
[70] Morris (1992), 105 (on the Bronze and Iron Age); cf. 385, on the archaic and classical periods.   [71] Hall (1992), 187–8.

entered from outside (and that was a great deal) was assimilated in a powerful and confident environment of closed-off monoglossia':[72] Bakhtin's large generalisation about classical Greek culture is over-stated, but it catches something distinctive, and something distinctively different from Roman culture.

My second, related, point is the unprecedented nature of that remark-able moment in the last third of the third century BCE, when the Romans enlisted foreign allies in their project of appropriating another people's literary culture in order to create their own vernacular literature – the first time that this had happened in Europe, and an event which made it possible for later European societies to have a literary history.[73]

If we put these two observations together, we will be able to see the Roman response to Greek myth not as something supine and impover-ished, but as one of many self-conscious strategies for arrogating power to themselves in their continual engagement with the Greek experience.[74] At the most basic level, everyone knows that Greek myths were an indispensable part of the Roman fashioning of their culture and their literature. They could not have a hellenising culture and literature with-out the myths: it simply was not an option. No myths, no literature; no literature, no culture – and the Roman elite, for some unfathomable complex of reasons, did want an equivalent to the culture of the Greeks.[75] If they wished to insert themselves into the pan-Hellenic sys-tem of mythic culture, they needed to do it in the same way as the members of any individual *Greek* state on the margins of the Greek world.[76] Like those other states, the Roman city had its own little stock of local myth, but it was the sharing of mainstream stories from the great store of pan-Hellenic knowledge that was demanded by the major genres, and that alone could give substance to the Romans' extraordi-nary ambition of becoming the first outsiders to lay claim to this alien patrimony.[77]

---

[72] Bakhtin (1981), 66–7.   [73] Above, pp. 52–3.

[74] If memory serves, I owe most of this paragraph to a conversation with Robert Kaster.

[75] Gruen (1990), 82–4, for speculation on their motives at the end of the First Punic War.

[76] *Mutatis mutandis*, one might detect a parallel in the Romans' systematic adoption of coinage a generation before: 'Coinage was a Greek device, and the Romans' adoption of it marks a conscious effort on their part to enter the cultural milieu of the Hellenistic world', Cornell (1995), 397.

[77] Cf. the observation of T. Hölscher in Graf (1993a), 187 n.48.

We should see this as an act that bestows power, not removes it. And it bestows power not only on the Romans but, potentially, on any subsequent culture. For the history of myth in Europe is a history of coping with the Roman, not the Greek, experience: when Lamberton says that 'our concept of a corpus of European literature with its origins in archaic Greece is a modern construct', one could substitute 'Roman' as the penultimate word.[78] This history is one of tapping into something which we have marked off as not *ours* but which we can, or must, make *ours*. Hence the central role of Greek myth in defining Roman culture, 'for the central, essential, paradox of that culture was precisely its simultaneous *incorporability* within Greek norms and its insistent *refusal* to construct itself in those terms'.[79]

The contact zone

At the risk of being accused of constructing my own myth of origins, I would view this paradox as a legacy of the first interstitial generations, when those tri-lingual *semigraeci* explored the crevices between the competing cultures of central and southern Italy.[80] We should not underestimate the cognitive power generated in these 'contact zones', as they have been labelled by Pratt, who chooses the term in order 'to foreground the interactive, improvisational dimensions of colonial encounters', looking at intercultural relations 'not in terms of separateness or apartheid, but in terms of copresence, interaction, interlocking understandings and practices, often within radically asymmetrical relations of power'.[81] Within the contact zone, in a dialectic described as 'mimesis and alterity' by the anthropologist Michael Taussig, interacting cultures are selecting from each other characteristic features for disparagement or envy.[82] A process of imitation most economically makes these features

---

[78] Lamberton (1986), 10.

[79] Beard (1993), 63 (original emphasis).

[80] Bakhtin was fascinated by the energy and creativity of this period, seeing it as an anticipation of Rabelais' world: Bakhtin (1968), 470–2 and (1981), 61–3. Note West's speculation that the transference of Eastern mythology to Greece was the work of 'a certain number of bilingual poets, probably easterners who had settled in Greece and learned to compose epic in the Greek manner': West (1988), 171.

[81] Pratt (1992), 7; cf. Greenblatt (1991), 4 on 'the inbetween, the zone of intersection'; and White (1991), on the 'middle ground'.

[82] Taussig (1993). I am much indebted to Neil Whitehead for discussions of his work in progress on 'mimesis and alterity' in colonial encounters in the New World.

available for experimentation and analysis, allowing one to capture and control the strange power of the other culture. As the alien features are brought home, the resulting sense of anxiety or revulsion produces a backlash, in which the imitated characteristics are once again set at a distance. The competing cultures, then, oscillate between concentrating on otherness, by focusing on what is different about their rivals, and concentrating on similarity, by the imitative process which best enables them to define and master what makes up that otherness.

Dynamic, interactive models of this kind are more valuable than the usual notions of 'influence' or 'borrowing'. First of all, they enable us to guard against the idea that the Romans are doing all the work in 'taking over' or 'using' Greek myth. The Greeks are energetic partners in this transaction from the beginning: the vicissitudes of the Trojan myth, for example, by means of which Greeks and Romans may be cast as either relatives or aliens, are clearly the product of a continual dialogue rather than an imposition of a grid by one party or the other.[83] In general, most studies of Roman hellenisation concentrate on the traffic in one direction only, rather than thinking in terms of a 'dynamic tension that structured both cultures'.[84] Again, it is much easier to make sense of the diversity of Roman engagement with Greek culture if we envisage a contentious and volatile contact zone rather than a developing process of assimilation. Assimilation is difficult to assess except in ameliorative terms, whereas Roman attitudes to Greek culture span the widest possible gamut, from admiration and envy to contempt and fear.[85] The Romans desire Greek *paideia* in order not to be at its mercy, and systematically imitate it; yet the very action of imitation keeps provoking them into the uneasy awareness that this *paideia* is not native, so that a complex process of inclusion and exclusion is always under way.[86] Part of the attraction of Greece for the Romans is that it can be a screen against which to project all that is un-Roman. In this way, the most rabid Hellenophobe finds that he cannot escape from the Greek, who is indispensable to his self-fashioning. In sum, there is no essence of Roman identity to which

[83] Gruen (1992), 6–51.

[84] Woolf (1994), 135 (on the Imperial period); see the important discussion of Curti-Dench-Patterson (1996), 181–8.

[85] The concentration on assimilation as a positive factor is the main drawback of the indispensable study of Gruen (1992).

[86] Wallace-Hadrill (1988).

extra Hellenising bits are added; rather, what counts as Roman identity is always being reconstructed under new interactive pressures.

Above all, if we are considering the mobility of myth between cultures, the dynamic model I have been suggesting is more helpful than the traditional one, which tends to see myth as fundamentally grounded in the society, as something already given which reflects upon societal norms which are themselves also already given. Edmunds' response to the fact that Near Eastern myths migrated to Greece illuminates the difficulty which the traditional model poses:

> This peregrine quality is in contradiction to the accepted concept of myth as possessing particular validity for the society that tells it. On that principle, a myth ought to be tied to a particular society and thus fixed. How could that society's beliefs, embodied in that myth, become another society's beliefs?[87]

These myths look a bit more like folklore, says Edmunds darkly, with recourse to one of the disparaging antitheses which the Hellenic model must produce in these circumstances. But if we think in terms of the dynamics of the contact zones, we may see that it is precisely the lack of exact 'fit' which makes the appropriation of myth attractive and viable. In the operation of myth even within a given society, Smith has suggested that 'there is delight and there is play in both the "fit" and the incongruity of the "fit"';[88] how much more powerful this fascination with 'application and inapplicability', with 'congruity and incongruity' must be when it is being generated in the interstices between cultures.

Studies of the contact zone may also help us conceptualise the potent general results which could flow from the Romans' ability to see the Greeks and their systems as simultaneously same and different. Greenblatt has written of the European 'mobile sensibility' which was generated in the contact zones which sprang up between Western Europe and the New World, and the implications of this 'mobile sensibility' have been lucidly summarised by Slater:

> One understands the thought of another not as a perception of truth but rather as an ideological, therefore constructed, therefore manipulable system. Although the other understands his own perception as simple truth, one possessed of the 'mobile sensibility' stands

[87] Edmunds (1990), 142.   [88] Smith (1978), 206.

outside of this perception and can therefore manipulate and control the other.[89]

The Romans, in other words, could see the Greek mythical system as a system, in a way that the Greeks themselves could not (one should probably say 'pre-Hellenistic' Greeks here, since the Hellenistic world from which Roman literature grew was one with its own sense of distance from a pre-existing and codified body of classical mythological texts). The resulting sense of simultaneous distance and closeness not only made the Greeks 'good to think with' for the Romans, and not only enabled the *semigraeci* even to contemplate the hubristic ambition of interacting with Greek literary culture as they did (at once collaborating in it, adding to it, and departing from it) – it also made it possible for them to take a synoptic view from vantage points denied to insiders. The Romans had been participants in Greek mythic systems for centuries, after all, but they were also observers, and it is possible that their very status as observers endowed their control of Greek myth with another kind of analytical power.[90]

Ovid's system

The great system in Roman mythography is Ovid's encyclopedic *Metamorphoses*, imperial in its totalising ambition. The poem's systematic and synoptic nature makes its status as myth precarious according to the Hellenic model: we have already seen that, according to Burkert, the poem approximates rather to folklore as a result of the fact that it eschews the cultic and social dimension of the original Greek myths.[91] Instead of responding, however, by trying to find ways in which Ovid's poem might be made to conform to the Hellenic model's definition of 'myth', we should consider the new work to which Greek myth is being put in this new context.

---

[89] Slater (1993), 120, referring to Ch. 6 of Greenblatt (1980). Slater is not using Greenblatt for my purposes, and I can therefore freely qualify 'simple truth' in my quotation as being not at all applicable to how the Greeks ever thought of their systems.

[90] Peter Bing alerts me to the importance of stressing that 'another kind of analytical power' does not mean a 'superior' kind: by no means do I wish to imply that an Alcaeus or a Euripides 'was so trapped in his own (primary) culture that he could not manipulate myth with any degree of analytical power' (*per litteras*).

[91] Burkert (1979), 24 (above, p. 63).

Ovid certainly does systematically remove from his accounts of metamorphosis almost all the cultic and regional *aetia* of his Greek sources,[92] but this is not because he has no interest in the local or ritual contexts of myth. On the contrary, while he is composing the *Metamorphoses* he is simultaneously composing a poem on precisely such aetiologies, the *Fasti*; and in the 'Italian' books at the close of the *Metamorphoses* he gives his readers a battery of myths which function as aetiologies of contemporary local practices (Hippolytus/Virbius, for example, becomes the attendant of Diana of Aricia, 15.545–6; Aeneas becomes *deus Indiges*, 14.607–8).[93] His regular amputation of such elements from his Greek myths, then, is not accidental or inadvertent, but part of a systematic dialogue between work on Greek and work on Roman myth. For it is by no means the case that in his eyes 'all myths were the same', so that he 'does not distinguish between Greek and Roman and eastern, between historical myths and local legends and tall tales'.[94] Ovid's distinctions are not necessarily the ones a modern source historian would make, but his treatment of aetiology in particular is an index of how concerned he is to maintain these categories as separate elements of his audience's inheritance.

In paring away the aetiologies of his Greek myths, his purpose is not to turn them into simple stories without a context, fictive opportunities. Rather, he wishes to concentrate on what he is progressively constructing as a new universal set of criteria for human behaviour, one which – so he will have it – has always been immanent in Greek myth but never 'properly' explicated before or brought into a system.[95] In his treatment of sexuality, in particular, a bewildering range of Greek myths comes to form a newly comprehensive anthropology, which provides a flexible structure within which to examine the ways humans define and experience themselves and others.[96]

The first story of passion is a vital one, marked as archetypal and programmatic with the introductory words 'first passion' (*primus amor*,

---

[92] Graf (1988), 60–2; Forbes Irving (1990), 29; note the important qualifications of Graf's position made by Myers (1994), 94.

[93] Graf (1988), 61–2; Myers (1994), 95–132.   [94] Solodow (1988), 75.

[95] Important study in Schmidt (1991), esp. 70–8.

[96] Feeney (1991), 195–8; Schmidt (1991) puts the traditional interest in Ovid as a poet of human psychology on a new footing with his account of Ovid's 'Psychologie als anthropologische Hermeneutik' (17–19).

1.452): within the economy of the poem as a whole, this is the moment of 'transition from cosmogony to mythological narrative'.[97] Apollo, having just shot the monster Python full of arrows, mocks Cupid for his undersized little bow, and Cupid asserts his mastery by shooting Apollo with a sharp arrow of gold to inflame him with love for Daphne, while shooting Daphne with a blunt arrow of lead to make her impervious (1.453–73). Apollo's first reaction to Daphne straightaway reveals his radical lack of interest in her and his obsession with his own kind of order, as he looks at her unkempt hair and immediately wishes to change her style: *'quid, si comantur?' ait* ('"How about if it was done up properly?"', he says', 1.498). He chases her as she runs away, speaking ceaselessly as he goes, expressing his incredulity that she is not as interested in him as he is: *non incola montis, | non ego sum pastor . . .* ('I am not a mountain-dweller, I am not a shepherd . . . ', 512–13). The only reason she is not responding must be that she does not know who he actually is: *nescis, temeraria, nescis, | quem fugis, ideoque fugis* ('You don't know, you thoughtless girl, you don't know who it is you're running away from – that must be why you're running away', 514–15). In order to enlighten her, he itemises all his accomplishments and cultic grandeur. His self-praise becomes a hymn to himself, transforming the hymn's usual insistent *second* person pronouns into a barrage of first persons, as a token of his utter lack of interest in that second, other, person, and his utter absorption in his own person:[98] *mihi . . . me . . . me . . . meum . . . nobis* (515–22). The Delphic god has absorbed only too well his most famous precept, Γνῶθι σαυτόν ('Know thyself'): already in the *Ars amatoria*, Apollo had urged 'knowing thyself' as the key to intelligent love-making (2.497–501).

As he catches up with her, Daphne successfully prays to her father for release, and is transformed into the laurel; Apollo still loves her under this guise, and inflicts on the wood kisses from which the wood shrinks (553–6). Now, finally, instead of apostrophising himself, he apostrophises her, with a list of the associations she will have with him for eternity; the hymnic second person now resounds in formal correctness, at the point when she is not 'you' any more, but his own attribute (557–9):

[97] Knox (1986), 14.
[98] Knox (1990), 200, on the formal transformation; cf. Wills (1990), 154.

'at quoniam coniunx mea non potes esse,
arbor eris certe' dixit 'mea. semper habebunt
te coma, te citharae, te nostrae, laure, pharetrae . . . '

'But since you can't be my wife, you'll definitely be my tree', he said.
'Thee my hair shall possess, thee my lyres, thee – o laurel – my quivers
. . . '

Standing as it does as the archetypal story of male sexuality, this devastating exposure of Apollo's maniacal self-obsession cuts away from any
specific or explicit links with the Greek cultic associations of Apollo and
his laurel.[99] Ovid's treatment, however, remains intimately dependent
upon the resonances of Greek accounts of the relationship between god
and tree. The idiotically perky pride in her Apollonian associations
which the loquacious laurel displays in Callimachus' *Iambus* 4 is rewrit-
ten so that it is now Apollo's pride, not the laurel's: Ovid's laurel will be
mutely suffering the god's impositions for eternity. Forbes Irving's discussion of the various Greek stories linking deities and plants finely
shows how 'the transformation into a tree . . . enables the heroine in plant
form to be both a lover of the god and yet to retain her virginity and
purity';[100] Ovid stifles this ameliorative possibility with his suffocating
image of speechless and immobile envelopment.

Apollo's address to the laurel is not finished, however. His speech
continues, to become the poem's first prophecy, taking the consequences
of the myth down into the time of the poet and his audience (560–3):

tu ducibus Latiis aderis, cum laeta triumphum
uox canet et uisent longas Capitolia pompas.
postibus Augustis eadem fidissima custos
ante fores stabis mediamque tuebere quercum.

Thou shalt attend on the leaders of Latium, when the joyous voice
shall sing the triumph song and the Capitoline Hill shall view the long
processions. And thou shalt also stand as a most trusty guardian at the
doorposts of Augustus, in front of the entrance, gazing at the oak
wreath in the middle.

[99] Graf (1988), 62. As Myers (1994), 62 points out, Ovid does mention at the beginning
of the story that the victors at Apollo's Pythian games at first received oak garlands,
since the laurel did not yet exist (1.445–51); formally, then, Daphne's transformation is an aetion for this practice, yet the emphasis of the narrative is entirely
elsewhere.   [100] Forbes Irving (1990), 136.

Daphne will become not only Apollo's but Augustus' laurel, a permanent token of the varied forms of the will to power.

Just as the first narrative of the poem uses its first simile to look forward to the time of Augustus, providing a frame for the entire movement of the poem, so this first story of sexuality uses the poem's first prophecy to project itself forward into the social and political context of the contemporary audience.[101] In this way Ovid shows that the mythic work of his poem is universalising, rather than universal, for its transcultural energy is not loosely mobile, but situated precisely within a new time and a new place, the empire of Rome. His bold act of translation in redefining myth's value and meaning for his own culture became paradigmatic for later acts of translation into other contexts: 'The European imagination is a network of references that centers, to a large extent, on Ovid.'[102] It is tempting to see Ovid's anticipation of this possibility in the poem's epilogue. Here he shows that he knows he will live on beyond his contemporary reception (*uiuam*, 'I shall live', is the poem's last word), while Augustus will be one day absent (*absens*, the last word addressed to Augustus, 15.870).[103]

Secondary origins

The intellectual and social energy that went into Roman appropriation of Greek myth was immense, and it involved people in every culture within the Latin penumbra. From Livius Andronicus in the third century BCE to Claudian – himself another native Greek speaker – in the fourth century CE, Latin writers devoted themselves to generating meanings from Greek myth, and we have no reason to smother those meanings because the artists did not have an umbilical cord connecting them to the origin, whatever and wherever that was. Looking at how something works is always more important and interesting than looking at where it came from – and if a treatment of a myth calls attention to the issue of origin, then that is itself a function of the work the myth is doing.

If we define myth according to one model, with a natural, primitive,

---

[101] On the first simile (1.200–5), see Feeney (1991), 199–200, 209–20.

[102] Blumenberg (1985), 351. As a first step in following Daphne, note how Petrarch appropriates the self-referential nature of Apollo's passion in his passion for his Laura, the 'laurel' who will make him the 'laureate': Freccero (1975).

[103] I owe the antithesis between *uiuam* and *absens* to Stephen Hinds.

almost instinctive mythopoesis springing from an idealised Greek organic experience, then we not only do no sort of justice to the Romans,
we also do no sort of justice to the Greeks. Worse, we disable all
subsequent Europeans and any of their inheritors. Graf quite rightly
stresses that analogies forward in time are bound to be more instructive
for the study of Roman myth than analogies back in time, so that
comparisons with post-Classical reception of myth will be potentially
very fruitful for students of Roman work on myth.[104] In the Renaissance,
after all, the Roman and Greek myths saturated the imaginative and
intellectual outlooks of the educated classes, producing a marked variety
of 'brain-balkanisation', since the official Christianity of the time was
incomparably more monolithic in its truth-claims and totalising in its
social ambitions than any pagan system. There are a series of contact
zones across time as well as space, in which later generations are induced
to make their own contribution to the dialogue between Greek and
Roman myth.

Let my alternative origin myth, then, be that of the Romans as
founders of an active and dynamic trans-cultural sensibility.

[104] Graf (1993a), 5, with preliminary bibliography.

CHAPTER

3

Divinity

Even ten years ago a chapter on 'divinity' in a book on Roman literature and religion would have appeared decidedly anomalous. There are gods everywhere in the Romans' city and literature, but according to the long-dominant models of Roman religion, the problem of the gods as entities, and of how to represent or engage with them, did not seem very pressing in a Roman context. Amongst the Romans themselves, Varro could fantasise about a pure stage in their religion, before foreign influence, in which the gods were not even conceived of as anthropomorphic, and some moderns have had their own versions of such a theory.[1] Even after the modern abandonment of the view which saw Roman deities as essentially or originally unanthropomorphic *numina*, the problem of divinity continued to have little relevance in a system which was thought to afford the gods only vestigial personality, without so much as allowing them to be actors in native mythic narratives.[2] If such was the case for the principal gods, then surely the host of personified abstractions ('Peace', 'Virtue', and so on) could only be frigid and devoid of religious interest, while the multitude of little deities with minutely specialised duties were self-evidently ridiculous – who could take seriously divine creatures named 'Top-dresser', 'Hoer', 'Raker' (*Obarator, Occator, Sarritor*), or 'Getterdown', 'Smasher-up', and 'Burner' (*Deferunda, Commolenda, Adolenda*)?[3] Finally, majority opinion for a long time regarded with something close to scorn a category of divinity which was prominent in the late Republic and the Empire – namely, divinised humanity.

---

[1] Varro *Div.* fr. 18; against this view and its modern exponents, Cornell (1995), 161–2.
[2] Wissowa (1912), 9, 23–4.   [3] Ogilvie (1981), 12–13.

Such unconcern about the nature of divinity in Roman religion could easily adapt itself to the new circumstances of the recent revaluation of Roman religion. Roman religiosity now appeared so clearly to emphasise civic cohesion and public performance that an interest in areas of more apparently 'religious' import, such as the divine, could well continue to seem only marginally significant. Scholars influenced by a Judaeo-Christian tradition, which sees the nature of God or a personal encounter with Him as central to religious thought and experience, have been hard pressed to find anything of the kind in Roman civic polytheism; they have then pronounced the search to be pointless, or have redirected it on to mystery cults, or the supposedly more personal area of domestic piety.[4]

Again, the Greek counter-example appears to tell against regarding the Romans' activity in this area as significant. The impact on modern imaginations of the spectacular divine creatures of Greek mythology has made it inevitable that many scholars should see 'the gods' as the essence of Greek religion, and should detect a corresponding hole at the centre of Roman religion.

There are, as we have seen, serious problems involved in the assumption that the gods of Greek cult and piety were experienced through the medium of the mighty personalities with which they were invested in drama and epic; as Vernant puts it, 'the Greek gods are powers, not persons'.[5] Nonetheless, we may certainly observe differences in emphasis in the two intellectual cultures' treatment of the gods in their investigations into religion. The Romans' Greek predecessors and contemporaries were the heirs of a centuries-long philosophical and scholarly engagement with poetic representations of the divine, and this engagement was one in which the Romans participated only obliquely, for their culture did not share the compulsion to make sense of epic poetry which ultimately conditioned all this Greek activity. The difference in priorities is seen in the different ways that the two most famous Roman and Greek scholars of religion organised the systematic study of their respective

---

[4] North (1989), 605.

[5] Above, p. 24; Vernant (1983), 328. In such contexts, as Terry McKiernan points out to me, we must remember that the personality we look for in an ancient god is a modern one, complex and imbued with subjectivity; the personality sought by the ancients would have been in line with their own, more objective, notions of human personality (on which see Gill (1996)).

fields.[6] Varro's *Antiquitates rerum diuinarum* were organised around the institutions of the state, treating the priestly colleges, shrines, and festivals of Rome in twelve books, before arriving at the gods for the final three;[7] Apollodorus' *On the Gods*, on the other hand, was organised around the Homeric gods and their etymologies and qualities.[8]

We must, however, be cautious and specific in drawing conclusions on the basis of such a comparison. It is clear that Herodotus, for example, does not assume that the gods are the automatic point of departure when he investigates the religious activity of all the peoples he describes. Almost invariably he begins with cult, and 'it is the descriptions of the cultic institutions as they are seen which calls forth a discussion of the gods and not vice versa'.[9] In this regard, Herodotus' priorities are very close to Varro's. The example of Herodotus clarifies the fact that the difference between an Apollodorus and a Varro is, above all, one of organisation. When a Greek looked at the variety of religious tradition and behaviour in the Hellenic world, the only possibility of a synoptic view was provided – as Herodotus himself famously pointed out three hundred years before Apollodorus – by the system of relationships and powers organised in the pan-Hellenic poetic tradition, which originated in Homer and Hesiod:[10] 'it is they who created a divine genealogy for the Greeks, gave the gods their titles, apportioned their honours and powers, and gave a representation of their forms' (2.53.2). For a Roman writing about his own religious tradition, the system was provided not by texts of poetry with their vivid divine personalities, but by whatever categorisations could be teased out of the bewilderingly diverse facets of civic activity. Such a Roman is not in a very different position from a Greek who is writing about the religion of one state, rather than of all the Greeks: there were many Greek works on the religion of individual states, Athens in particular, and they too make the festivals and cults

---

[6] Feeney (1991), 106.

[7] Fr. 4; on the significance of this arrangement, see Turcan (1988), 2.5; Gordon (1990), 180.   [8] Pfeiffer (1968), 261.   [9] Smith (1978), 248.

[10] Nagy (1979), 7; Burkert (1985), 120; cf. Sourvinou-Inwood (1991), 148–50. It is interesting to note that the Greek Dionysius of Halicarnassus describes Romulus behaving very like Homer and Hesiod, fixing the gods' 'representations, symbols, powers and gifts' (*Ant. Rom.* 2.18.2), while the Roman Varro has one monarch after another introducing gods, concentrating on the cumulative and sequentially collaborative nature of the process: frr. 35 (Romulus), 36 (Titius Tatius), 37 (Numa).

their focus, not the gods.[11] If the Latin states had been as diverse, numerous, and widely-spread as the Greek ones, then a treatise on their religion would almost inevitably have had to take the deities as the organising factor as well.

Looking (harder) for the Other in Rome

If historically there have been various reasons for a comparative lack of interest in Roman divinity, there have been many recent signs of a new enthusiasm for the subject. The sheer range of number and type of divinities, after all, is very characteristic of Roman polytheism, and may help to explain some distinctive features of their religion – the rich elaboration of their ritual system, the ease with which they accommodated competing systems, and the lack of pressure for a consistent unifying theology.[12] A key injection of energy has come from the field of semiotics, creating an interest in the issues of the conceptualisation and representation of the divine.[13] Other recent studies have begun to concentrate on the 'otherness' of Roman divinity, working on the assumption that 'religion is only "religion" if it is about the other'.[14] There have been fundamentally important reassessments of the relationship between Roman gods and their worshippers, and of the problem of the divinity of human beings, in the form of the imperial cult.[15] Against the background of this rediscovery of a Roman relish for the issues associated with divinity, the lavish attention paid to the gods in Roman literature begins to look less and less like an anomaly, and it becomes necessary to reconsider the work that Roman literature is doing in this area of Roman culture.

No book on literature and religion at Rome, then, should ignore the issue of their constructions of divinity. If I now devote a chapter to this subject, however, I do not do so in order to redeem Roman religion as genuinely 'religious', as if only a profound interest in divinity will entitle a religious system to that dignity. It is often postulated that the core of

---

[11] Tresp (1914), 2–29.
[12] All these features are linked with a multiplicity of deities in the general model of religion offered by Lawson and McCauley (1990), 163–5.
[13] Important study in Gordon (1979); cf., e.g., Elsner (1995).
[14] Beard (1989), 57; cf. Elsner (1995), 171.
[15] Scheid (1990), 475–676 (sacrifices to Bona Dea); Price (1984).

any religion or religious experience is to be found in divinity, and especially in an encounter with the 'other'; and we have already remarked upon the power of this assumption in both a Judaeo-Christian and Hellenic context. But it is clear – to take one extreme – that systems do exist which most Western observers would wish to label 'religious', although they have virtually no recognisable divine agents or personalities, and show no interest in the problems of human encounters with members of another ontological realm.[16] Roman religion would still be analysable as a religion if it turned out to have been such a system – if it had been, in other words, rather the kind of system which Wissowa and many others have taken it to be. And yet the fact is that it was not such a system, as will emerge in our discussion. Roman interest in divinity was pervasive and various, and repays investigation, but our investigation should not be motivated by an assumption that divinity is what religion is all about, and that this is the key which will unlock the inner chamber of the Romans' religious experience – whether to reveal it as full or empty.

The neutral evidence of prose?

Let us begin with the authors of prose (speeches, letters, histories). I do not do so because these forms of literature are 'normal' or 'natural', offering an unfiltered view onto what was really thought: the argument of the first chapter should have alerted us sufficiently to the perils of overlooking the contextually defined rules of particular forms of speech. It is important to begin here precisely because such texts are often cited as proof of a pervasive lack of interest in the gods as personalised participants, and especially as proof of a fundamental rationalism among educated writers.[17]

Certainly, it is exceedingly rare for these texts to speak of personalised divinities at work, and when authors in these genres do allude to divine agency they will speak in vague and usually collective terms of the beneficent or malevolent action of 'gods', 'immortal gods', 'god', 'some god or other'. In Cicero's correspondence, for example, he and his

[16] Balagangadhara (1994), 286, on Western dilemmas over the categorisation of, e.g., Buddhism.   [17] E.g. Liebeschuetz (1979), 29–33.

friends use phrases such as *nisi quis nos deus respexerit* ('unless some god or other has a care for us', *Att.* 16.6); *qui illi di irati!* ('may the angry gods blast him!', *Att.* 77.1); *sed haec deus aliquis gubernabit* ('but some god or other will guide these matters home', *Att.* 117.3); *'di' inquis 'auerruncent!'* ('"May the gods ward it off!"', you [i.e., Atticus, an Epicurean] say', *Att.* 169.1); *a dis immortalibus ereptus* ('snatched away by the immortal gods', *Fam.* 187.4); *deum benignitate* ('by the kindness of the gods', [L. Munatius Plancus] *Fam.* 371.6). Similarly, historians may speak in imposing and sinister fashion of the *deum ira*, 'the anger of the gods', without telling us which particular gods were angry and why.[18]

So far from being proof of a peculiarly Roman lack of interest in the specifics of divine action and motivation, however, this pattern is entirely unsurprising in the light of ancient conventions. Indeed, it is more or less precisely the pattern to be found in classical Greece, where orators and historians speak in just the same vague way of 'the gods' or 'god', without specifying a particular deity.[19] Both in the Roman and the Greek worlds, it holds broadly true that the ordinary human in the ordinary course of events, without privileged access to knowledge of divinity's action, must necessarily speak in this general manner. From the beginning of the Greek tradition, poets and seers may speak of divinity's actions in a much more particularised way. But the difference we see in Greece between the more poetic and more prosaic modes is not the result of a change in theological outlook over time, for already in Homer we see a clear distinction between the characterful narrative of divine agents presented by the poet himself and the general talk of 'god' or *'daimon'* used by the human character Odysseus in his own narrative of his adventures.[20]

A significant departure in Roman habits of speech, however, is to be found in the fact that, whereas the prose sources of Athens speak of the gods as responsible only for beneficent actions, the corresponding Roman sources are full of talk of divine anger and retribution.[21] The

---

[18] Tac. *Ann.* 4.1.2, with Martin and Woodman (1989) ad loc.

[19] Mikalson (1983), 63–8; cf. Bloch (1963), 14, on the discrepancy in Greece between the mythical and cultic representations of divine intervention.

[20] Feeney (1991), 85–6; cf. Mikalson (1983), 112.

[21] Mikalson (1991), 18, on the Greeks; Bloch (1963), 86 on the difference between Greeks and Romans.

difference is ultimately to be explained by the anxiety concerning divine anger which underpins the Roman apparatus of prodigy and expiation.[22] As Jocelyn remarks, 'the Romans regarded all *prodigia* as signs of divine displeasure and fear was their automatic response': he makes the point most effectively by showing how Cicero adds the vital word *timidi* to the Greek original when he is translating Homer's account of how the army responded to the omen at Aulis.[23] The Roman historical tradition is accordingly replete with accounts of the Senate's response to the report of prodigies, as they attempt to placate the offended gods.[24] Oratory, like the other great performance genre, tragedy, will even represent the wicked as harried by divine agency, describing with zest the punishment inflicted on political opponents by the divine collective.[25] The seamless mesh of the religious and political in public life meant that it was a regular part of Roman political rhetoric to stigmatise opposing policies as disruptive of the *pax deorum*, the equilibrium between the human and divine orders, and to claim divine support for one's own policies.[26]

Such forms of speech are grounded in an assumption that the gods of the state have not only an interest and a will, but the means to make their will known and effective. The practices of augury and haruspicy certainly presuppose that a will is being expressed. The human authorities have to try to translate and interpret this will – hence Cicero's description of the augurs as *interpretes internuntiique Iouis Optimi Maximi*, 'interpreters and intermediaries of Jupiter Optimus Maximus', *Phil.* 13.12. Even more, they must try to control the divine will if at all possible.[27] Such images of the gods' interest and purpose occasionally make their way into oratory. In the *Catilinarians* Cicero speaks of Jupiter's and the gods' will being expressed to the citizen body (3.18–22); and he once even evokes a marvellous image of the Magna Mater, outraged at the pollution of her games, scouring the fields and forests with din and hubbub (*Har. Resp.* 24).

Although the divine collective is regularly attended to in these forms of literature, then, a concern with a particular deity is fairly rare,

---

[22] Linderski (1986), 2228, on the cautious suppositions underpinning the augural law; cf. 2202 n.198.   [23] Jocelyn (1973), 105–6, on Cic. *Div.* 2.64 and Hom. *Il.* 2.320.

[24] Bloch (1963); Levene (1993), on Livy's use of this tradition.

[25] E.g. Cic. *Har. Resp.* 39; *Pis.* 46 (with Nisbet (1961) ad loc.).

[26] Liebeschuetz (1979), 50–1; Beard (1994), 745–9.

[27] North (1976), 6–8; Scheid (1985), 51–3; Linderski (1986), 2207; Beard (1990), 36.

occasioned by the fairly rare moments when a particular cult and its deity are pressingly at issue. Even then apology may be necessary, as when Cicero excuses himself in the *Verrines* for speaking at such length of the myth and cult of Ceres in Sicily: *uereor ne oratio mea aliena ab iudiciorum ratione et a cotidiana dicendi consuetudine esse uideatur* ('I am afraid that my oration may look inappropriate to the norm of the lawcourts and everyday habits of speech', 2.4.109). The comparatively exiguous interest in particular divine personalities shown in such sources, however, is strikingly incongruent with the highly elaborated interest on display in other contexts, not least that of cult. The city had a great number of different deities, types of deities, and ways of representing those deities – yet the sources we have been discussing so far allow barely a glimpse of all this complexity. This incongruity is not to be brushed aside as no more than one would expect from the magpie mentality of the Romans. Once again, we are very close to the position which Mikalson describes in Athenian religion, where we similarly find, side by side, 'the appeal to a large number of particularized gods in cult settings and the conception of an undifferentiated collective of gods in a noncult setting'.[28]

In Rome, as in Greece, the important work of speculating and fantasising about the divine was overwhelmingly concentrated in areas other than those we have been considering so far. To lay the ground for an investigation into the part other forms of literature had to play in this work, we need to have some grasp of what this 'large number of particularized gods in cult settings' was like in Rome; we need a brief taxonomy of the Romans' representation of divinity in cult settings.[29]

A taxonomy of divine representation in Roman cult

As generally in the urban civilisations of the Mediterranean, the dominant figures of cult were gods housed in temples. The canonical image of cult was the anthropomorphic statue of the god, inevitably represented with such human features as gender, and endowed with characteristic attributes, which might be peculiar to the individual shrine or shared

[28] Mikalson (1983), 72 – although he regards this as a 'paradox' which 'is a distinguishing feature of Athenian popular religion' (73).
[29] Very helpful taxonomy in BNP, 'Gods and Goddesses, old and new'; cf. Latte (1960), 50–61.

with images of the god in other shrines.[30] These images of divine power
and personality often dated back to the first years of the Republic, and
must have had an impact on Roman conceptions of divinity just as
pervasive as that which such images had on the Greeks.[31] Turcan makes
this point well by citing the words of Cotta, the sceptical Academic
spokesman in Cicero's dialogue *De natura deorum*, who, when arguing
against the anthropomorphism of the Epicureans, has to concede that it
is natural for Romans to conceive of the gods as they are represented in
the images which adorn their shrines (1.81):[32]

> nobis fortasse sic occurrit ut dicis; a paruis enim Iouem Iunonem
> Mineruam Neptunum Vulcanum Apollinem reliquos deos ea facie
> nouimus qua pictores fictoresque uoluerunt, neque solum facie sed
> etiam ornatu aetate uestitu.

> In our case the situation is perhaps as you say it is; for from childhood
> we know Jupiter, Juno, Minerva, Neptune, Vulcan, Apollo and the
> other gods with the particular face which painters and sculptors
> wanted them to have – and not just the face, but even the adornment,
> age, and clothing.

The 'painters and sculptors' mentioned here by Cotta were, of course,
Greek, and had been since the 490s BCE, when Damophilos and Gor-
gasos embellished the shrine of Ceres with paintings and terracotta
statues, as advertised by Greek verses on the shrine, which announced
that Damophilos had done the work on the right hand side and Gor-
gasos the work on the left (Plin. *HN* 35.154).

The anthropomorphic deity with personal name and attributes was
not the only form in which Roman cult conceptualised divinity. Some
deities were anthropomorphic yet generic, retaining the same undifferentiated labels and attributes wherever they were found: any house could
have its own Lares, Penates and Genius.[33] Just as in the Greek world,
certain natural or man-made objects were worshipped as divine, al-

---

[30] Burkert (1985), 88–92; Turcan (1988) 1.11–12, on the distinctive attributes of
Roman cult-images; Varro *Div.* fr. 228, on temples and statues as the defining
attributes of the public gods of the Roman people.

[31] On the impact of cult images on Greek concepts of divinity, MacMullen (1981), 31;
Lane Fox (1986), 153–4.   [32] Turcan (1988), 1.8.

[33] Orr (1978), 1562–75; outside the house the Lares and Genius could have epithets
added to specify their role.

though the nature of this divinity was – and remains – highly problematic.[34] Further, a multitude of little powers could be listed in prayer, although they were never represented in imagistic form, and were encountered in no other context than this rare form of liturgical incantation.[35] These *Indigitamenta* had significant names which bespoke their minutely specialised function (*Vaticanus* makes the child cry, *Cunina* looks after him in the cradle, *Potina* gives him drink), and ancient Christians and modern scholars alike have had much hilarity at their expense, since they seem to encapsulate both groups' hostile view of Roman religion as pettifogging and unspiritual. Such an approach is all too typical of the way in which the marginal elements of Roman religion have been elevated into the characteristic. In fact, such creatures are not a substitute for a more fully realised divine personality, but function as the entourage of that personality, clustering around the great god as the mob of slaves, parasites, freedmen and friends clusters around the Roman aristocrat.[36] We shall be saying no more about the *Indigitamenta*.

Personifications – as they are conventionally but clumsily labelled – make up an important and conceptually challenging category in the cult of the Roman, as of the Greek, city.[37] To modern readers they are a difficult class, for the long tradition of hostility to allegory and personification allegory in particular has left us in a peculiarly weak position when it comes to appreciating such forces. From early on, certain qualities, forces or states appear to have been honoured by the Romans as divine, to be worshipped in the hope that the power inherent in their name might be attracted if beneficent (Ops, 'Produce'), or averted if malevolent (Robigus, 'Grain Rust'; Febris, 'Malaria'): we may note that the deification of 'bad' qualities was a notorious scandal to the philosophers.[38] Early, likewise, are some cults of entities which modern readers would recognise most readily as 'personifications', such as Concordia ('Harmony', 'Concord') and Salus ('Salvation', 'Safety'). The great ma-

[34] Dumézil (1970), 23–8; cf. De Visser (1903), 54–156 for the Greek analogies.

[35] Dumézil (1970), 36; Turcan (1988), 1.6; see Usener (1896), 247–73, for the analogous minor heroes and daimons of Greece, with cross-reference to the *Indigitamenta* (273).

[36] Dumézil (1970), 33–8; for the *turba* of the god, see McKeown (1989), on Ov. *Am.* 1.1.5–6.

[37] Deubner in Roscher (1884–1937), 3.2.2127–45; Fears (1981), with 830–3 on terminology.   [38] Cic. *Nat.D.* 3.63 with Pease (1955–58) ad loc.

jority of such personifications, however, entered Roman life and cult in the same wave of Hellenising religious innovation which we have already remarked upon in Chapter 1, during the spectacular 'long century' in which the Romans exploded from the status of central Italian to Mediterranean and Asian power (300 – 188 BCE).[39] These were the years which saw the introduction of, for example, Victoria ('Victory'), Spes ('Hope'), Fides ('Faith'), Libertas ('Liberty'), Mens ('Intelligence'), Virtus ('Courage', 'Virtue'). Based on the cults of the Greek states, these new deities were established at the command of the Sibylline Books, and were worshipped *Graeco ritu*: at the shrine of Honos ('Status', 'Distinction', 'Honour'), for example, you might witness something so completely unRoman as the sight of a female victim (a cow) being sacrificed to a male deity.[40] The new cults were clearly extremely popular, and for the governing class they were a powerfully flexible way of negotiating between Greek and Roman values and ideologies at a period when such negotiation was of the highest importance to the expanding empire.[41] Once more, we see how it was religious contexts that offered the most supple and attractive venue for the articulation of novel ideologies – although the tenacious primitivist tendency in the study of Roman religion is interestingly illustrated by the frequent attempts to backdate into an early pre-Greek phase those personifications which appear most alluringly to embody archetypal Roman qualities (Fides, Virtus).[42]

The personifications were to come into their own again in the service of another novel religious ideology, that of the emperors.[43] At this point we meet our last principal category, for the city not only honoured divinities whom everyone knew had once been human, but also honoured the living emperor within the context of other divine cult, and with forms derived from the cult of gods.[44] The deification of humans was and is an enormously controversial and complex topic; at the end of this chapter we shall investigate some of the ways in which Roman writers grappled with its conceptual and artistic challenges.

If these are the main categories of divinity, they do not exhaust the

---

[39] Fears (1981), 846–9; above, pp. 51–2.   [40] Fears (1981), 858–9.
[41] Fears (1981), 849, 859 and Gruen (1992), 101 represent the first steps towards an investigation of this fascinating phenomenon; Axtell (1907), 69–70 and Fraenkel (1960), 216, on the popularity of these cults in Plautus.
[42] Fears (1981), 846 n.76.   [43] Fears (1981), 889–938.
[44] Price (1984) and Chs. 4 and 7 of BNP.

bewildering subdivisions on which the Romans could lavish attention (*di certi, incerti, praecipui et selecti, nouensides, indigetes, consentes* . . .). All these divine categories were much debated by the Romans from early on in their literary and scholarly tradition.[45] Categorisation of divinity was likewise on display in civic cult, for every year in the procession of images before the games the citizen body could see different kinds of divinities clustered together: the details are uncertain, but the *pompa* certainly included the major gods of the state (Jupiter, Juno, Neptune, and so on), as well as demi-gods such as Hercules, Aesculapius, and the Dioscuri, and 'personifications', such as Victoria.[46] The language of prayer similarly shows a responsiveness to the wide range of divine possibilities: a Roman would occasionally say 'by whatever name you wish to be called', 'whoever you are', 'whether you are male or female'.[47] Such phrasing is a token of a quirky recognition that the net which humans try to throw over the creatures swimming in that other medium is a net of human manufacture, which we can never be entirely confident has the right-sized mesh.[48]

In the recognition that our own net is a rough and ready one, let us cast it over the various forms of representing and engaging with divinity, especially in literature. First, we shall consider the personifications, for the other categories represent more of a continuum, and are best treated in sequence. After the personifications, then, we shall examine the personalised major gods and their images, and move, via epiphany, to the interaction of gods and humans; we may then conclude the chapter by tracing back up the ladder again, to investigate the divinisation of humans.

Personifications

These cults presented – as they still do – vexing problems of definition. Are Pax, Virtus, and so forth attributes of divinity, or divinities in themselves, or divinised attributes of humanity, or intrinsically human qualities which remain human, or human counterfeits of divinity?[49] At *Fast.* 6.92, Ovid packs almost all of these interpretative possibilities into four words, when he describes Concordia as *placidi numen opusque ducis*, 'the divinity and work of the mild leader'. She is a divine force that

[45] Rawson (1985), 289.   [46] Dion. Hal. *Ant. Rom.* 7.72.13; Ov. *Am.* 3.2.
[47] Alvar (1985).   [48] Dumézil (1970), 43–6.
[49] Cic. *Nat. D.* 2.79, 3.61, *Leg.* 2.28; Varro *Div.* fr. 189; cf. Wissowa (1912), 327–8.

inspires Augustus from outside; she is a divine force that springs from Augustus; she is the 'work' of Augustus because he refounded her divine cult; she is the 'work' of Augustus because as a political leader he discharges and embodies the function of harmonious concord.

From a modern point of view, the problem of abstracts seems to be compounded by the Romans' lack of a distinction between majuscule and minuscule letters. Thinking about the difference between *Pax* and *pax* is not easy, but it would appear to be a good deal easier than thinking about the difference between *PAX* and *PAX*. The clarity enforced by modern printing conventions, however, may obscure the advantages accruing to a mentality that did not rigidly impose demarcations between words, qualities, and instantiations, and that could fruitfully mobilise this indeterminacy in an improvisational spirit.[50] As often, a Plautine joke beautifully illustrates the possibilities,[51] and illustrates likewise how the recognition of these possibilities was inherent to the system from the start of our literary evidence.

Towards the beginning of *Bacchides*, when the young man Pistoclerus is going indoors for a party, the slave Lydus asks him who lives in there, and gets the reply 'Love, Pleasure, Venus, Venusness, Joy, Joke, Fun, Chat, Lusciouskissitude' (*Amor, Voluptas, Venu', Venustas, Gaudium, | Iocu', Ludus, Sermo, Suauisauiatio*, 115–16). In this long list of abstracts, 'Venus' of course stands out as a 'real' goddess, but Plautus personifies her quality by juxtaposing her with the cognate word for 'charm', *uenustas*, 'the quality of being Venus-y'; he may also be making us retrospectively wonder whether Amor is a noun or the name of the son of Venus. The slave asks Pistoclerus why he's having any truck 'with gods that are so bad for you' (*cum dis damnosissumis*), hilariously involving himself in the problem we touched on above (p. 85), of how bad qualities can be divinised. The young man indignantly chastises the slave for speaking ill of the gods, provoking the marvellous question: 'Is Lusciouskissitude any god?' (*an deus est ullus Suauisauiatio?*, 120). Pistoclerus rounds on him for being so ignorant about divine nomenclature at his age (*stultior es barbaro poticio, | qui tantus natu deorum nescis nomina*, 123–4), but the old man's question has revealed the apparent randomness behind the whole operation, since any imposing abstract word can indeed look awfully like a divinity in the right context.

---

[50] Fears (1981), 845 n.69.   [51] Axtell (1907), 71.

At one level, of course, the issue is clear-cut. As another Plautine joke already makes clear, divinity is having a statue and an altar and receiving sacrifice, and in this regard some 'abstracts' were gods and some were not.[52] Yet the line could be blurred. In Horace's *carmen saeculare*, for example, all of the personifications are bracketed off in their own single stanza, as if to call attention to this one particular category of divinity (*Fides, Pax, Honos, Pudor, Virtus, Copia*, 57–60): this isolated grouping corresponds to the practice of cult, which never joined personal and abstract deities.[53] Out of this list, however, Pudor ('Modesty', 'Shame') attracts attention because the name of 'Modesty' in Roman cult is not the masculine Pudor but the feminine Pudicitia. Pudicitia, however, will not scan in Sapphics, and Horace clearly feels entitled to allude to the actual cult name by means of a cognate abstract, even if that abstract does not itself receive cult, and is of a different gender. The quality of the divinity is in the root of the word, not in a particular form, or a particular temple.

While scholars, then, may mark which abstracts had – so to speak – a capital letter as the objects of civic cult, there were many grey areas. The useful study of Axtell (1907), for example, divides the deified abstracts into 'State-Cults', 'Abstracts popularly but not officially worshiped', 'Occasional and individual deifications', 'Doubtful examples'. The essentially improvisational frame of mind which is behind the state's recognition of a quality as divine cannot be confined to the civic sphere, and artists may innovate *ex tempore* just as private citizens did. Horace, again, in his hymn to Fortuna of Antium (*C.* 1.35), introduces various personifications into her train. Two of these, Spes and Fides, belong with Fortuna in Roman cult, and Fides is even pictured imitating the action of her official priests, with her hand wrapped (21–2).[54] The sinister figure of Necessitas, however, is not a figure of cult (17–20): she is the Greek Ἀνάγκη, here transformed into a Roman slave, equipped with the terrifying instruments of official mutilation and death (nails, wedges, hooks, and molten lead).[55] Axtell, as many others, is troubled by the

---

[52] *si quidem mihi statuam et aram statuis | atque ut deo mi hic immolas bouem: nam ego tibi Salus sum, Asin.* 712–13; cf. Varro fr. 190: *Felicitas dea est. aedem accepit, aram meruit, sacra congrua persoluta sunt.*

[53] With the exception of Aesculapius and Salus: Axtell (1907), 93.

[54] Nisbet-Hubbard (1970), 395–6.

[55] Following West (1995), 172–3; for her Greek origin, Nisbet-Hubbard (1970), 395–6.

collocation of 'a mere concept of the imagination' and 'an actual deity', and this parade of abstractions is regularly chastised as frigid;[56] yet Horace's improvisational importing of the Greek 'Necessity' vividly actualises the range of Fortuna's crowd of attendants, capturing the mixture of the appalling and the dignified that would have characterised the entourage of the magistrate en route to the chastisement of a malefactor. Further, the cultic status of Fortuna herself is something of an issue in this context, for the hymn to Fortuna is preceded by a poem in which we encounter fortune 'without a capital letter', as a general force, in tension with Jupiter the Thunderer and the doctrines of Epicurus (1.34). The 'tyche' of Hellenistic thought modulates into the civic goddess of Roman cult: the two poems offer two different statuses for the 'same' name.[57]

There are interesting problems involved in figuring such qualities as persons in order for them to be objects of cult. They have to be gendered, for a start, if they are to have a statue, and the gender of the abstract noun inevitably dictates the gender of the deity. One result is that neuter abstracts such as *auxilium* ('Aid') cannot become gods – a point which Plautus plays upon with another fine moment of comedy at the beginning of the *Cistellaria*, when the inept figure of personified 'Auxilium' blunders crossly onto the stage 150 lines into the action, grumbling because his (its?) role as the divine Prologue who (which?) explains the plot has been preempted by the soliloquy of one of the characters (149–153). Another result of the gender convention is that practically every one of these deities will be feminine, not simply because many Latin abstract nouns are feminine, but because practically every Greek one is, and so many of these Roman deities come from Greek.[58] The divine force, therefore, which embodies pure masculinity is grammatically and iconographically feminine – *Vir-tus*. Statius, for one, finds the anomaly piquant, as he introduces the outlandish figure of Virtus onto his Theban battlefield (*Theb.* 10.639–46): she tries to make herself more feminine, moving away from her masculine connotations by disguising herself as a woman in order to persuade the Theban hero Menoeceus to

---

[56] Axtell (1907), 68.

[57] See Nisbet-Hubbard (1970), 387 for the difference between Tyche and the Roman Fortuna.

[58] Only Honos ('Status'. 'Honour') and Bonus Eventus ('Good Outcome') were masculine in gender and iconography.

withdraw from the battle and commit an expiatory suicide.[59] Her attempt to assimilate herself to her grammatical gender only highlights the oddity of her traditional function as the embodiment of masculinity: such moments open up a fundamental crevice in the whole convention, revealing that there can never be a total overlap between the general idea of the quality and its particular manifestation.

In order for their special characteristics to come into perspective, it is crucial to see these deities as part of a larger system of divinity, in tandem with the other gods of the state. Neither category of divinity supersedes the other: at moments of crisis and innovation the state sets up new divinities from each category, so that we see the military catastrophes of Hannibal's invasion, for example, leading to the simultaneous establishment of new cults of Mens ('Intelligence') and Venus of Eryx on the Capitoline in 215 BCE (Liv. 22.9.10 and 10.10). The example of Concordia illustrates one particularly important way in which the divinity of the personifications differs from that of the other gods. It is striking that a number of different shrines and temples were established for Concordia over a long period of history.[60] When some great moment of concord occurred, the state did not necessarily avail itself of an existing temple to pay her honour for this new benefit, but consecrated a new temple to acknowledge her instantiation on this occasion. Ovid reveals the mentality behind such homage when he notes Tiberius' rebuilding and rededication of Camillus' old temple of Concordia: *causa recens melior*, he says (*Fast.* 1.645), 'the recent cause was the better', showing how the separate instantiations of Concordia were separately marked, linked to a specific manifestation of her quality in the human realm.

As Whitman well puts it, the personifications 'emerge from an emphasis on *human* conditions'.[61] They are a means of projecting human qualities 'upwards' so that they may partake of another sphere's capacity for power, from where they may then be invoked and drawn 'downwards' again. Jupiter, Juno and the other individualised gods, on the

---

[59] Feeney (1991), 382–5.   [60] Wissowa (1912), 328–9.

[61] Whitman (1987), 272 (original italics); cf. Feeney (1991), 390–1, and Kuttner (1995), 21 on the shrines of Honos and Virtus established by Marius and Pompey being 'more a way for the victorious military patron to say something about his own achievements than the expression of reverence for a deity already receiving continuous worship'.

other hand, have their own (often inscrutable) personalities and will, and remain more independent of human categories. The difference is clearly shown by the fact that the personalised gods are not associated with particular groups by means of modifying genitives, as the personifications may be. The sense of identity of this group or that may be expressed by dedications to 'the Concordia of the people of Agrigentum' or 'of our guild', but the major personalised gods do not attach such groups to themselves in the genitive.[62] Such a distinction should not automatically be read as a sign that the personifications are an inferior form; rather, seen as part of a flexible and intelligent system, they may be apprehended as one of the specialised ways of conceptualising and harnessing the power of divinity that was available to state, group, individual, and artist.

Anthropomorphic, personalised gods

(i) *the State's representations*

As we noted at the beginning of the chapter, it was possible for Varro to claim that there had been a long phase in Roman religion before anthropomorphic divine representation. He went further, saying that the gods would now be worshipped in a more pure fashion if this custom were still in force (*quod si adhuc . . . mansisset, castius dii obseruarentur, Div.* fr. 18). So far from being the folk-memory of a primitive indigenous state which it has sometimes been taken to be, however, Varro's stance represents the Romanising of an old and sophisticated Greek intellectual tradition, which posited an idealised early period when the people of Greece worshipped the gods without images.[63] True divinity has neither gender nor age nor distinct bodily limbs, according to the standard philosophical line;[64] the folly of representing the divine in anthropomorphic iconography had been a commonplace of the philosophers for centuries before Varro, as had been the concomitant theory which held that the anthropomorphism of state cult was a device to intimidate and curb the lower orders.[65]

---

[62] Axtell (1907), 89.
[63] Burkert (1985), 88 n.53 has references to the Greek tradition.
[64] Varro ap. August. *De civ. D.* 4.27 (Cardauns (1976), 1.37); Plin. *HN* 2.14.
[65] Feeney (1991), 6–7 (anthropomorphism); Cardauns (1976) on Varr. *Div.* fr. 18 (the political motive).

By the time of the poet Lucilius in the late second century BCE, a century before Varro, all these views were already current in Rome, as is shown by some remarkable lines satirising contemporary superstition (fr. 484-9 Marx):

> terriculas, Lamias, Fauni quas Pompiliique
> instituere Numae, tremit has, hic omnia ponit.
> ut pueri infantes credunt signa omnia aena
> uiuere et esse homines, sic istic omnia ficta
> uera putant, credunt signis cor inesse in aenis.
> pergula fictorum ueri nil, omnia ficta.

The bogies and witches that your sylvan oracle-mongers the Fauni and your King Pompilius Numas instituted, he trembles at them, and stakes everything on them. As children before they can speak believe that all bronze statues are alive and are human beings, so those (*deluded adults*) think that all the moulded objects/fakes/fictions are real, and believe that there is intelligence inside the bronze statues. The shop-front of the makers/fakers has nothing real, all moulded objects/fakes/fictions.

Lucilius may have a reputation for prolixity, but in these few lines he puts his finger on a remarkable number of important issues concerning the representation of the divine in state cult.[66] Lucilius pokes fun at the conventional 'super-human but still recognisably human' portrayal of the gods by saying that children fall into two category-mistakes. First, they think that the statues are alive, when they are of course inanimate; but they also think that they 'are' humans, when some of them 'are' really gods. But the category-mistake of the superstitious grown-up is much worse, for he is confusing the representation of a god with the god, believing that the intelligence of divinity is tucked away within the bronze container as snugly as Lucilius' word for intelligence is tucked away within his words for bronze containers (*signis COR inesse in aenis*). The superstitious grown-up is lacking intelligence as much as the statue, and we contemplate an animate human without intelligence contemplating an inanimate god without intelligence: the human viewer and the divine viewed end up, once again, having more in common than one

---

[66] The text of 487 is dubious: the context of iconography inclines me to accept and print L. Mueller's emendation, but see O'Hara (1987) for an alternative.

might like to think. The last line of our fragment confuses two other categories, those of cult and art: the images are all the products of workshops, to be displayed and purchased as merchandise, whether they represent the human or divine.[67]

This problem of the relationship between the gods and their represen-tations has been much discussed for many periods and places in the ancient world.[68] It is important to realise from the outset that when Roman literary artists engage with such issues they are not performing an interesting operation upon a given set of flat and static forms of behaviour, for Roman state cult itself shows an inventive and varied zeal in exploring the conceptual problems associated with divine images. As Gordon well puts it, 'people believed simultaneously that statues were gods and that they were not'; he describes the resulting attitude as a 'game of "let's pretend they are gods" which the Greeks (and the Romans) played with their statues and other representations of divin-ity'.[69] In some ways the gods are conceived of as occupying their own dimension, independent of their representation by the city: in augury, for example, they are imagined as facing south, regardless of the orientation of their temples and images.[70] Yet the cultic representation of the gods in the city is a way of binding them in civic life, anchoring them as fellow-citizens who partake of the time and space of the other citizens.[71] Cicero explicitly contrasts Greek and Roman cult with Persian on this score. The Persians may have thought the Greeks mistaken to shut up gods within temple walls, on the grounds that everything should be open and free to the gods, whose temple and abode was the whole world; 'but the Greeks and we Romans have a better way, for our wish, in order to promote piety towards the gods, has been for the gods to inhabit the same cities as us' (*easdem illos urbis quas nos incolere uoluerunt, Leg.* 2.26).

---

[67] Cf. Gordon (1979), 11, on the Romans' reclassification of Greek 'offerings' as 'art'.

[68] Gordon (1979); Lane Fox (1986), 102–67; Versnel (1987); Faraone (1992). Contem-porary Hindu cult likewise has a sophisticated interest in the problem of the ontological status of divine images: Waghorne and Cutler (1985).

[69] Gordon (1979), 16–17; cf. Versnel (1987), 46–7.

[70] Linderski (1986), 338, on the evidence of Varro preserved in *Ling.* 7.6–7 and Festus 454L.

[71] Catalano (1978), esp. 445; Scheid (1985), 51–5. Again, Hindu conceptions are very close: 'As cohabitors of a common spatial and temporal plane of being, gods and humans are involved in mutual interactions', Cutler in Waghorne and Cutler (1985), 168–9.

A fragment of Senecan diatribe against superstition, preserved by Augustine (*De civ. D.* 6.10), offers a fascinating insight into Roman attitudes to the embodiment of divinity in statuary. Seneca describes the bedlam on the summit of the Capitoline hill, and tells us of the host of minions attending on the grandees of the Capitoline triad (Jupiter, Juno, and Minerva). Jupiter has someone to announce his visitors' names, says Seneca, and someone to tell him the time. But the next servants described for Jupiter (and Juno and Minerva as well) stand out as a good deal more bizarre, captured by Seneca in the act of playing out an intricate imitative game of make-believe:

> alius lutor est, alius unctor, qui uano motu bracchiorum imitatur unguentem. sunt quae Iunoni ac Mineruae capillos disponant (longe a templo, non tantum a simulacro stantes digitos mouent ornantium modo), sunt quae speculum teneant.

> One is a bather, one an anointer, who with a mime-action of his limbs imitates someone anointing. There are women who do Juno's and Minerva's hair (they stand a long way from the temple, not just from the statue, and move their fingers in the manner of people dressing hair), there are some who hold the mirror.

These people are not tending to the needs of the gods, for the gods have no needs. But neither are they even tending to the needs of the statues. If the gods will pretend to be embodied in the statue, pretend to have unkempt hair and dry skin and eyes to see 'their' own image thrown back at them in the mirror, then the humans will pretend to tend to 'them' in the statue. The behaviour of these devotees is a dramatic example of how lucidly the Romans could reflect upon the limits of the mimetic forms with which they honoured their gods. The physical embodiment is not commensurate with the divinity, but the very lack of commensurability powerfully suggests the grandeur of divinity's uncontainable force.[72]

In his study of the banquets of the Arval Brethren, J. Scheid has given a fine account of how self-conscious state ritual could be about the fictive nature and fictive power of its negotiations with divinity. The banquets offered by the Arval Brethren to the gods are arranged in such a way as to highlight the fact that the dining experience is not 'real', and that the

---

[72] Gordon (1979) is indispensable to the whole topic.

statues of the divinities are not themselves the participants: the effect is to evoke the presence of the deity, while expressing 'the otherness, superiority, but also solidarity of the divinity'.[73] The Romans regularly invited the gods to share such banquets with them, in a ritual called the *lectisternium*, where images of the gods were reclined on couches like Roman citizens.[74]

The city's most elaborate display of the gods' images was in the procession before the games, the *pompa circensis*. The gods were brought out of their homes (*aedes*), and carried on special litters (*fercula*) to view the games and be viewed themselves, while their attributes (*exuuiae*) were transported in carriages (*tensae*).[75] Many categories of divinity were paraded here, in a uniquely Roman spectacle whose energetic splendour is faintly preserved in some dynamic reliefs.[76] As the principal venue for display of divinity, the *pompa* could arouse high emotions, and was necessarily adaptable to changes in ideology: there was a riot when Octavian and Antony removed the statue of Neptune, the favourite god of their rival, Sextus Pompeius; and Caesar's introduction of his own statue into the *pompa* was the first step in the imperial appropriation of the pageant.[77]

One of the most striking aspects of the *pompa* is the double parade of the gods' images and their attributes: Jupiter would be represented not only by a statue carried by four men, but by his thunderbolt in a carriage. The difference has sometimes been explained as the result of historical development, with iconic forms coming later than attributive ones.[78] But the two types of representation are in dialogue with each other, in a way that is reminiscent of the fictive play underlying the *lectisternium* of the Arval Brethren. Two different conceptions of divinity and its representation are on display here, for the deity is embodied in the statue, but represented by synecdoche in the attributes.[79] When the gods' images are brought out of their temples, the conception of them as fellow-citizens is at work – perhaps with an extra degree of mimesis, since the image that is

[73] Scheid (1990), 670.   [74] *RE* 22.1108–15 (Wissowa); Latte (1960), 242–4.

[75] Latte (1960), 248–50; Long (1987), 239–42.

[76] Turcan (1988) vol. 2, figs. 50–52. On the rarity of such processions of images in Greece, see Burkert (1985), 92.

[77] Dio 48.31.5 (Neptune); Dio 43.45.2 (Caesar), with Fishwick (1987–92), 555–6 on later developments.   [78] Latte (1960), 249 n.2.

[79] On the difference, see Gordon (1979), 13; Price (1984), 184.

paraded may be a portable image of the massive cult image itself.[80] The throng of divine effigies represents the gods as present, manipulable, assimilable to human norms, like us; their physical participation is mimicked as they are brought out of their homes, manoeuvred into position so that they have a good view, and so on – here above all one sees the power of Taussig's insight that 'the making and existence of the artifact that portrays something gives one power over that which is portrayed'.[81] The parade of divine attributes, on the other hand, is a way of alluding to and symbolising the gods' non-human power: this strategy represents the gods as absent, uncanny, unsnareable by direct human mimesis.

Anthropomorphic, personalised gods

(ii) *Literature's representations*

The writers of Roman literature show an intense interest in the problems of the representation of divinity, for they are not only members of a civic culture that compulsively stages and re-stages the categories and attributes of divinity, but honorary members of a Greek poetic and intellectual culture that had concerned itself with these issues for centuries.[82] Already in Homer, 'a constant poetic preoccupation . . . is the question of how far divine power is susceptible to the narrative accommodations which are the indispensable medium for capturing that power – and this preoccupation mirrors the recurrent pagan insistence on the "contradiction and ambiguity" which are inherent in the "predictable and unpredictable, human and non-human" divine'.[83] Poets must accommodate divinity to the forms of language, just as the state must accommodate it to ivory or marble.

Virgil reveals how deeply these forms of mimesis can be implicated in each other when he describes how Aeneas is beautified by his mother Venus as he meets Dido, in a moment like that of epiphany (*Aen.* 1.588–93):

[80] Long (1987), 242; though see Fishwick (1987–92), 554 for another interpretation.
[81] Taussig (1993), 13.
[82] For the background, and for discussions of the issues in Homer, Apollonius, Virgil and Ovid, see Feeney (1991), 45–52, 69–80, 165–71, 233–5. My discussion here is a supplement to that fuller account.
[83] Feeney (1991), 51, with references to Gould (1985), 24, 32.

restitit Aeneas claraque in luce refulsit
os umerosque deo similis; namque ipsa decoram
caesariem nato genetrix lumenque iuuentae
purpureum et laetos oculis adflarat honores:
quale manus addunt ebori decus, aut ubi flauo
argentum Pariusue lapis circumdatur auro.

Aeneas stood there and shone in the bright light, similar to a god in
his face and shoulders; for his mother had inspired her son's hair with
grace, and breathed upon him the purple light of youth, giving joyous
lustre to his eyes – grace such as hands add to ivory, or when silver or
Parian marble is surrounded by yellow gold.

Virgil says that Aeneas is 'similar to a god', but his elaboration of that
analogy moves through the intangible divine aura of graceful light and
lustre (which he shares with his divine mother, *rosea ceruice refulsit*,
1.402) to a simile which likens Aeneas' appearance to that of statuary.[84]
To the question 'What is a god like?' comes the answer 'Like a statue of a
god'. The attempt to describe what a god is like defers the problem of
representation, short-circuiting through the divine dimension back into
another dimension of mimesis, that of state cult.

   As this interchange between different forms of mimesis shows, divinity
is ultimately incommensurate with *any* form of human representation.
Philosophers had been preaching this point for centuries, yet their efforts
did not curtail discussions of which form of mimesis might be more
adequate to the divine nature, or halt experiments in capturing its unique
power. Phidias' statue of Zeus at Olympia can catch something of divine
intelligence, as Dio Chrysostom points out in our most extended comparison between poetic and iconic mimesis of divinity; yet it does so by
analogy with the human form's function as a vessel of intelligence, while
the poet may represent this intelligence in speech and action (12.58–9,
62). The licence of the poet is far greater than that of the sculptor (64–6),
and the poet may therefore represent all manner of divine manifestations
which the sculptor cannot match: striking and awe-inspiring manifesta-

---

[84] Henry (1873–92), 1.773–7 establishes that a statue is the referent. Aeneas' similarity
   to a god is an allusion to the prophecy of *Hymn. Hom. Ven.* 200–1, but the statuary
   alludes to the state cult of the Caesars: the verbal cue of *caesariem* (590) is picked up
   immediately by *genetrix*, the cult title of Venus in Julius Caesar's Forum, where a
   statue of the dictator also stood (Plin. *HN* 34.18).

tions of power such as the lightning, rainbow, shooting star (which may, indeed, be out of harmony with the lofty beneficence which Dio wishes to see embodied in Phidias' statue, 78).

Poetic mimesis of divinity, then, remains self-conscious about the fact that its manner of representing divinity is an accommodation, with its own powers and failings. This is true even in the case of a single divinity, which may be so various, and may embody so many different powers and meanings, that capturing it in words may seem intractable. Ovid explores the issues in his long section on Vesta's feast day in the *Fasti* (9 June; 6.249–348).[85] His treatment is involved with a rich tradition of debate about the problems of representing Vesta. What was the best way to represent her? Was she, indeed, or could she be represented? What actually was in that round temple of hers, and what did it signify?[86] Ovid's discussion becomes a poetic corollary to the state's twinned strategies for representing divinity, by icon and by synecdoche.

At the beginning of the section the poet shows himself in prayer, and then, instead of conversing with a god as he so often has already in the work, he becomes aware of a divine power that communicates with him although he does not see it or hear it (6.251–6):

> in prece totus eram: caelestia numina sensi,
>   laetaque purpurea luce refulsit humus.
> non equidem uidi (ualeant mendacia uatum)
>   te, dea, nec fueras aspicienda uiro;
> sed quae nescieram quorumque errore tenebar
>   cognita sunt nullo praecipiente mihi.

I was lost in prayer: I felt the influence of celestial divinity, and the glad earth gleamed with a purple light. Not that I saw you, goddess – away with the lies of bards! – you were not one to be seen by a man. But the things I did not know, concerning which I was held in error, were understood without anyone giving me information.

Vesta here is both unspeaking and unspeakable, an unrepresentable absence, who yet has power. She is inaccessible to the poet because she is a virgin and he is a man, yet her unrepresentability goes deeper, for she is a force of nature – in fact, she is two forces of nature, earth (267–82) and fire (291). Earlier in his poem, Ovid may have mistakenly reported a

---

[85] Cf. Barchiesi (1994), 193–8.   [86] Beard (1995).

tradition that images of Vesta reacted with horror to the rape of the Vestal Virgin Silvia (3.45–6, *feruntur*); now he knows better, and reports that there are no images of Vesta or of fire within her temple (295–8). The fire really is fire, and does not need to be represented; Vesta does not need to be represented either – unless it is the fire that performs that function, or the hearth (300–8), or her temple, shaped round like the earth (279–82).

Ovid's presentation suggests that Vesta's strange essences may best be captured by synecdoche. Yet he knows full well that if she is to be a character in narrative other accommodations are inevitable, and his treatment of Vesta's feast day is capped by a mythic narrative in which a perfectly anthropomorphic Vesta is almost raped by Priapus (6.319–44). Elsewhere in the poem Vesta does speak (3.699–702, addressing Ovid; 6.467–8); and elsewhere Ovid refers to the image of Vesta in Augustus' Palatine residence (6.425–6).[87] Already in the Republic coinage had shown a representation of the image of Vesta, and the custom continued under the Empire.[88] Ovid refers to Vesta's status as patron goddess of bakers (6.311–18), and Ovid's readership would have been familiar with a fully anthropomorphised Vesta in this context, for on domestic wall-paintings she is shown leading or riding the miller's donkeys.[89] Ovid's evocation of Vesta's unrepresentable powers on her feast-day is not, then, the final 'truth' about Vesta, even within the context of his own poem. As the conscientious religious poet, he takes the controversial status of Vesta as a starting point for exploring one of the important ways of speculating about divinity current in his culture.

Literary interest in these great problems of divinity and its representation is no late development in Roman literary history, but is evident from the start of their literary tradition – as one might expect, given the remarkable atmosphere of religious improvisation and innovation into which the new literature was born. The sheer variety of possible ways of figuring and imagining divinity is an important part of the tradition from the beginning. Ennius translated from Greek two works which had quite incompatible explanations of divinity, *Epicharmus* (the gods are natural physical phenomena) and *Euhemerus* (the gods are former humans honoured for benefactions).[90] He worked all this into his epic poem, the

---

[87] Barchiesi (1994), 195, 198.   [88] Turcan (1988), 1.3–4.
[89] Orr (1978), 1561, 1580.   [90] Feeney (1991), 120–2.

Annales, where he also described the institution of state cult by King Numa (114–18 Sk.), and gave an account of at least one *lectisternium*. When listing the twelve gods honoured in the *lectisternium* of 217 BCE, Ennius deliberately adopts a bald and official style which must – although we can no longer recover this – have been dynamically in tension with the manner in which these same divine personages were characterfully represented in the Homeric manner elsewhere in the poem: *Iuno Vesta Minerua Ceres Diana Venus Mars | Mercurius Iouis Neptunus Volcanus Apollo* (240–1 Sk.).[91] The bare names are lined up without comment or elaboration in the verses just as the inert effigies are lined up on the couches.

Any one work may contain numerous different ways of conceiving of a single divinity.[92] Modern readers may consider such variety to be incoherent, yet Virgil's Juno, for example, gains rather than loses power as a result of the manifold ways in which her colossally threatening malevolence may be figured.[93] Let us close this section with a consideration of how a lyric poet puts the many facets of a divinity to work; let us consider the patron goddess of Horace's fourth book of *Odes*.

The book opens with Venus initiating hostilities against Horace once again after a ten year truce since the first collection of *Odes* (*Intermissa, Venus, diu | rursus bella moues?*). The power of Sappho is very strong at this point, for the prayer to the goddess of love, and the rueful 'once again', take us back to Sappho's Hymn to Aphrodite (fr.1), with its repeated 'once again' (δηὖτε, 15, 16, 18).[94] This hymn stood at the beginning of Sappho's collected works in the Alexandrian editions, so that the allusion signals the achieved monumentality that will be a consequence of this apparently uncontrolled opening, while the self-referential language of 'once again' alerts us to the revivifying of the model: Venus is visiting Horace once again, and Aphrodite is visiting a great lyric love poet once again.[95] Venus' attempt to revive her Sapphic role as lyric love goddess from the first collection is marked by the

[91] On the style, see Skutsch (1985), 424–5.

[92] Feeney (1991), 124 for the multiple nature of Ennius' Jupiter.

[93] Feeney (1991), 130–42.

[94] Putnam (1986), 39–42, on Sappho; A. Barchiesi pointed out to me the importance of 'once again', and of the position of Sappho's poem in the collected works.

[95] On such 'reflexive annotation', see Hinds (1998), Ch. 1, 'Reflexivity: Allusion and self-annotation'.

repetition of a phrase from a poem in the first book, where Horace was already struggling to escape from her influence – *mater saeua Cupidinum* ('savage mother of the Cupids', 4.1.5 = 1.19.1). Horace attempts to deflect her onto a more fitting target, the youthful, noble, articulate, and wealthy Paulus Maximus (9–20). She will be commemorated by Maximus, promises Horace, in the form of a marble statue by the Alban lakes: *Albanos prope te lacus | ponet marmoream* (19–20). Horace here plays upon the multiple meanings of *ponere*, and upon the ancients' frequent elision of the words 'statue of': 'he will place you in marble form/erect a marble you'. The vulgar confusion of the deity and its representation is humorously followed up in the next lines, when Horace tells Venus that she will inhale lots of incense there with her *nostrils* (*illic plurima naribus | duces tura*, 21–2), and enjoy listening to a variety of songs in her praise sung by choruses of girls and boys (22–8).

Venus' bizarre and sensuous incarnation in the statue of Maximus acquires extra resonance as the book goes on to develop its interest in the tussle between the media of statuary and poetry.[96] In 4.8 Horace disavows statuary's (and painting's) forms of representation, using this same word for representation, *ponere*, as he distances himself from the Greeks Parrhasius and Scopas, 'this one by means of stone, that one by means of flowing colours skilled to place/portray/erect now a man, now a god' (*hic saxo, liquidis ille coloribus | sollers nunc hominem ponere, nunc deum*, 4.8.7–8). Maximus' manner of representing Venus would be fixed, committed to a fallacious kind of physicality, a mirage of embodied presence; Horace's own representations of her will be a hundred times more powerful.[97]

Not only the manner of representing Venus changes after the first poem, however, for the 'savage mother of the sweet Cupids', the menacing figure of love lyric, will be changed by the final poem into a different kind of mother, with different offspring: in the last line of the book, Horace promises collective song of 'Troy and Anchises and the offspring of nurturing Venus' (*Troiamque et Anchisen et almae | progeniem Veneris canemus*). The book takes us from private hymns in honour of a marble love goddess to public Horatian lyric in honour of a civic and imperial

---

[96] Fine discussions of this theme in Putnam (1986); Hardie (1993b); Barchiesi (1996).
[97] See *C.* 4.2.19–20 for a justification of my multiple.

goddess whose persona is apprehended through the *Aeneid*, and through the *Aeneid*'s appropriation of Lucretius.[98]

This development begins in the next poem in which we meet Venus after the opening. In 4.6 we see her acting as an agent of divine and imperial history, joining Apollo in winning Jupiter around to helping Aeneas resettle the remnants of Troy in Italy (21–4): here we find her not *saeua*, 'savage', as in the first ode, but *grata* (21) – pleasing to Jupiter and in his favour. After this glimpse of her Virgilian role as a suppliant for her son and his people, two more poems trace the transience of the power she incorporates as a love goddess. In the tenth ode Horace addresses the boy who had entranced him in the opening poem, saying that he is still cruel and powerful with the endowments of Venus (*O crudelis adhuc et Veneris muneribus potens*, 4.10.1). But that time will pass, and soon he will see 'another you', *te . . . alterum*, when he looks in the mirror (6), and it will not be the usual 'other you' we normally see in the mirror; then he will find himself saying 'alas, why?' just as Horace had in the first poem (*heu . . . cur . . . cur*, 4.10.6–8; *cur heu . . . cur . . . cur*, 4.1.33–5). In 4.13 Horace addresses Lyce, who has advanced even further, into old age. The son of Venus runs away from her (*refugit te*, 10), and so does Venus herself: 'where is Venus running away to, alas?' (*quo fugit Venus, heu . . . ?*, 17). Where Venus is running away to is the last line of the last poem of the book. Here, as we have already seen, she emerges as a nurturing mother, not a savage one, and her child is not Cupid, but Aeneas, and his descendant, Augustus. The prayer for peace which Lucretius addressed to Venus at the beginning of *De rerum natura* has finally been answered:[99] war is at an end and peace does reign, and Venus has become genuinely 'nurturing', *almae*, as in the second line of Lucretius (*alma Venus*).

This sketch of Venus' meanings in the fourth book allows us to see something of the power that may come from the interaction between the various ways of figuring her divinity. She is the love force of archaic lyric and of Horace's own earlier reworkings of archaic lyric; she is a philo-sophical principle of generation recast as a political and historical one; she is a force to be addressed by the poet or remotely projected into the future as an ongoing object of civic celebration, and thereby a figure for

[98] Putnam (1986), 295–9.
[99] Putnam (1986), 295–6; 4.15 also answers Horace's own prayer in 1.2, where Venus and Mars are juxtaposed as possible authors of peace (33–40).

the trajectory of his own career. To do any of this work she must be captured in one medium or another, and Horace argues that his medium can capture and preserve more of her than the authoritative medium of statuary, for all its beauty and apparent immediacy and permanence.

Divinity may ultimately elude the various attempts of artists or states to categorise and contain it, but the attention that Virgil and Horace pay to the variety of Juno's or Venus' capacities is not a sign of confusion. We should respect their recognition that the manifestations of a god are necessarily local and contingent. The poems Juno and Venus inhabit are now one of those manifestations, just as a statue or a painting: the cultural set of possible representations, possible ways of apprehending them, now includes this work.

Crossing the line

(i) *Epiphany*

Many of the most interesting problems associated with divinity are to be found at moments when the divine crashes through the barrier between its own medium and ours, in epiphany.[100] Once, according to a prevalent nostalgia, that barrier was not there. Even a civic philosopher could say that 'antiquity was closest to the gods' (*antiquitas proxume accedit ad deos*, Cic. *Leg.* 2.27), and historians and antiquarians, with varying degrees of generic scepticism, could report distant occasions when gods dined with humans, or mingled with them in sex or battle.[101] There were more recent reports as well, most commonly of divine assistance in battle, and the status of these epiphanies in the historical record was keenly debated: Cicero's interlocutors in *De natura deorum*, for example, wrangle over the many famous epiphanies of the Dioscuri.[102]

To poets, the fantasy of such a time was very potent. Before the dreadful demarcation of the end of the Golden Age, according to Catullus at the end of his 'Peleus and Thetis', 'in former times the

---

[100] Pfister in *RE* Suppl. 4.277–323; Lane Fox (1986), 102–67; Versnel (1987).

[101] Dion. Hal. *Ant. Rom.* 1.77.3 (Mars and Ilia); Paus. 8.2.4–5 (Zeus and Lycaon); Liv. *Praef.* 7; 1.7.4–12 (Hercules and Evander).

[102] 2.6, 3.11–13, with Pease (1955–8). See Pritchett (1976), 11–46 for a collection of 'military epiphanies'. The standard public line is that gods do not communicate via epiphany, but prodigies (Cic. *Har. Resp.* 62), which are practically the voice of Jupiter Optimus Maximus (ibid., 11).

heaven-dwellers used to visit heroes' chaste homes in their full bodily presence and show themselves to mortal gathering, when piety had not yet been spurned' (*praesentes namque ante domos inuisere castas | heroum, et sese mortali ostendere coetu, | caelicolae nondum spreta pietate solebant*, 64.384–6). Once the age of sin began, and humans expelled Justice from their mind (397–8), human crimes caused the just mind of the gods to turn from us (405–6); the collapse of this meeting of minds led to the end of the meeting of presences: *quare nec talis dignantur uisere coetus, | nec se contingi patiuntur lumine claro* ('therefore they do not deign to visit such gatherings, nor allow themselves to be touched by the clear light of day', 407–8). No more visions of divinity, then, of the kind that graced the light of day when Argo sailed at the beginning of the poem, the last day of the Golden Age (*illa, atque haud alia, uiderunt luce marinas | mortales oculis nudato corpore Nymphas*; 'on that light/day and no other mortals saw with their eyes Nymphs of the sea with bared bodies', 16–17).

Catullus introduces a finely Roman note into his cataloguing of the kind of divine presence that humans no longer experience. It is one of the cardinal differences between the lost Golden Age and the present that humans and gods no longer eat together,[103] and Catullus therefore introduces a picture of Jupiter dining with humans as the first of his vignettes of the intimacy between humans and gods that existed before the age of sin: on his annual feast days 'the father of the gods, sitting in his shining temple, often saw a hundred oxen fall down on the ground' (*saepe pater diuum templo in fulgente residens | . . . conspexit terra centum procumbere tauros*, 387–9). But Catullus' words may simultaneously be read as a description of Jupiter's participation in the contemporary Roman cult of the *lectisternium*, or as 'Jupiter of the Feast', Jupiter Dapalis. The words, and the image of the god observing from his temple, are identical in either case; but then he was fully present, and now he has only whatever presence his statue may give him.

Now that the Golden Age of unmediated intimacy has gone, seeing a god is very dangerous, even fatal; already in Homer we hear a goddess saying that 'the gods are hard to cope with when seen very clearly' (*Il.* 20.131).[104] Stories abound of humans who are incinerated, maimed, or

---

[103] Hesiod, fr. 1.6–7; Gatz (1967), 36–7.
[104] Lane Fox (1986), 109–14 (his translation).

blinded when they encounter a god (Semele, Anchises, Teiresias, Saul). Usually, therefore, a god's appearance to a mortal will be mediated through dream or disguise, and Virgil reveals the close similarity of these strategies when he uses virtually identical language to describe a god appearing in a dream and appearing in a disguise (*omnia Mercurio similis, uocemque coloremque|et crinis flauos*, *Aen.* 4.558–9; *omnia longaeuo similis uocemque coloremque|et crinis albos*, 9.650–1). Only at the moment of the god's departure will there be a glimpse of their real divinity, as the illusory nature of the encounter is exposed (*Aen.* 1.402–5):[105]

> Dixit et auertens rosea ceruice refulsit,
> ambrosiaeque comae diuinum uertice odorem
> spirauere; pedes uestis defluxit ad imos,
> et uera incessu patuit dea.

Venus spoke and turning away shone with her rosy neck, and her ambrosial hair breathed divine aroma from her head; her dress flowed down to the bottom of her feet, and in her gait she was revealed as a true goddess.

As in this example, where Venus shuns direct conversation with her own son, we occasionally glimpse a view from the other side of the divide. Humans are commonly so terrified by epiphany that it is difficult to see the moment from the divinity's point of view, as potentially one of weakness and compromise. Divinity in these moments is accommodating itself to a realm for which it feels interest and even affection, but which ultimately remains ineffably inferior.[106] Hence the angry shame of Aphrodite in the *Homeric Hymn*, forced by madness into coupling with the mortal Anchises (198–9; 247–55); hence the peremptory refusal of Venus to involve herself in the grief of her son, fruit of that coupling (Virg. *Aen.* 1.385–6). When the gods mingle with humans in disguise, they may also avoid the complexities and risks of a true interaction. Plautus highlights the differences in what is at stake for god and human with his conversations between Jupiter, disguised as Amphitryo, and Amphitryo's virtuous wife, Alcmena. After the real Amphitryo has berated Alcmena for her apparent adultery, the disguised Jupiter returns

---

[105] For the departure as a common moment of revelation, see Richardson (1993) on Hom. *Il.* 24. 460–7.   [106] Griffin (1980), 179–204.

for more lovemaking. The whole scene revolves around his claim that he was joking, not in earnest, and her avowal of how much pain his joke caused her (903–22). The humour here is mordant, since ultimately Jupiter is telling the truth: in the end, it is all *iocus* to him, not *serium*.

Behind many accounts of epiphany one may detect a sense of the gap between the lost unmediated contact of a fantasised past and the murky encounters of the present, hedged about with the uncertainties of dream or vision or disguise. In Poem 68, Catullus memorably conjures up this gap with an epiphany of a human, his 'shining goddess' (*candida diua*, 68.70). The arrival of his beloved at the house where they will make love is compared to the arrival of a bride at the husband's house (73–4), and the atmosphere of epithalamium provides the point of departure for the comparison of his beloved to a deity, and of her arrival to an epiphany.[107] The implications of this equation are devastating, for Catullus' beloved is thereby endowed with a divinity's supreme unaccountability and ultimate unconcern for her mortal host:[108] her immense power to bless is twinned with an immense power to harm. Catullus pulls back from his equation at the end of the poem, with his deadpan remark that it is not right for humans to be compared to gods (141); and in his envoi he prays that his addressee may receive divine blessings of the kind once distributed by Themis in the Golden Age (153–5), reminding us of the kind of encounter which is gone for ever. These retractions ensure that the beloved hovers between the realms of mortal and divine, not fully assimilated to either, and recalcitrant to description as a result. The comparison with the liminal occasion of epiphany helps to focus the strange nature of the moment that the poem is trying to commemorate: it is a moment of transcendence (linking the beloved to a divine realm, and linking the two of them to the remote past with its glamorous and doomed heroes and heroines); and it is a moment of context-bound actuality (this threshold, this house). The beloved, then, is on the margin between all kinds of experience – actual and fantastic, mundane and romantic, human and divine. Above all, she is on the edge of representability.[109] That is the way in which she is most like a god.

---

[107] cf. 61.16–20 (the bride is like Venus coming to Paris); Edwards (1991); Feeney (1992), 33–4; Roberts (1989), on later epithalamia. In Hindu weddings, 'bride and groom are divine on their wedding day', Fuller (1992), 30.

[108] Finely argued by Edwards (1991), 73.   [109] Feeney (1992).

Crossing the line

(ii) *Apotheosis*

The fact that Catullus' human beloved is represented as a goddess leads us into the final category of this chapter, the divinised human. For all the remarkable distinctions between the divine and the human which we have been examining so far, the boundaries were at various times more negotiable than in some other religious traditions: 'there was no simple polarity, but a continuous spectrum, between the human and the divine'.[110] The philosophically inclined could postulate intermediate creatures called 'demons'; families and state alike maintained a cult of the dead ancestors – Cicero was elaborating on this tradition in his plans for a shrine to ensure apotheosis for his daughter, Tullia.[111] The same improvisatory mentality we saw at work with personifications could also express itself in the recognition of something divine in another person: Plautus' characters may flamboyantly hail their saviours as 'Jupiter'; the elegists create a mystique of the 'divine girl', *puella diuina*.[112] Lucretius' way of speaking about Epicurus shows how much nuance could be brought to the task of individual innovation. The hymn he addresses to Epicurus at the beginning of Book 3 has neither Epicurus' name nor an imperative, and therefore carefully refrains from using the precise forms of cult and imputing powers of intervention to the addressee; at the beginning of Book 5 Lucretius says that Epicurus *was* a god (*deus ille fuit, deus*, 5.8), and *appears* or *is seen* to be a god (*deus esse uidetur*, 5.19); while at the beginning of Book 6 Epicurus is called a man (*uirum*, 6.5), who has been carried to heaven by widespread ancient glory after his death on account of his god-like discoveries (*cuius et extincti propter diuina reperta | diuulgata uetus iam ad caelum gloria fertur*, 6.7–8).

Imputing divine qualities to a person is one thing; claiming that he is or will be a god is another. The state acknowledged that certain sons of

---

[110] Beard (1994), 750; cf. Toynbee (1947), esp. 126–9; Weinstock (1971), 291–3. See below, p. 110, for reservations about the use of this paradigm to neutralise ruler-cult. Cf. Fuller (1992), 3, on the way Hinduism, 'unlike Judaism, Christianity, and Islam,...postulates no absolute distinction between divine and human beings'.

[111] Demons: Burkert (1985), 331–2; cult of the dead: Weinstock (1971), 291–2; Cicero and Tullia, above, p. 19.

[112] Plautus *Pers.* 99, with Weinstock (1971), 292; *puella diuina*: McKeown (1989), on Ov. *Am.* 1.5.1–8.

gods were divine, gave them temples and paraded their images in the *pompa* (Hercules, Aesculapius, Dioscuri, Liber) – although while the Republic endured, as we shall see, no Roman received those honours apart from the founder of the city, Romulus/Quirinus. Even during the Republic Roman aristocrats might find themselves called upon to ponder whether a man could become a god. As a young senator of thirty-three, Cicero was on a senatorial advisory council asked to assess a dispute between the Roman tax-collectors and the people of Oropus, home to a shrine of the prophet Amphiaraus.[113] The *publicani* argued that the shrine should not be tax-exempt as a religious foundation, since Amphiaraus had once been a man and could not now be a god. The committee, however, recommended that the Senate rule in favour of the people of Oropus, as it duly did.

The main rupture, however, comes with the collapse of the Republic and the emergence of a revolutionary autocracy. As part of a re-orientation of the traditional Roman links between religion and exercise of power, the supreme ruler of the world was re-defined not only as a religious agent but as a religious personality. First the dictator Caesar, then his son Augustus and his successors, gathered the disparate threads of republican priesthood and cult into one rope, becoming members of all the priestly colleges, organising a religious policy, associating themselves with divinity in a range of contexts, and becoming the objects of carefully discriminated forms of cult all over the empire, which ideally culminated in their reception into the state's pantheon as *diui* after their death.[114]

Important recent accounts have stressed the continuity between the Republic and Principate in attitudes to human and divine links,[115] and it is undeniable that many concepts and practices underpinning the 'imperial cult' are visible even as early as the lifetime of Scipio Africanus: cases are on record where great Republican commanders received cult in the Greek East, claimed the patronage of deities such as Jupiter or

[113] Cic. *Nat. D.* 3.49, with Pease (1955–8) ad loc. on Dittenberg. *SIG* 2³.747.

[114] A personal selection of items I have found most useful in this massive topic: Weinstock (1971); Price (1984) and Chs. 4 and 7 in BNP; Fishwick (1987–92); Gordon (1990); Wallace-Hadrill (1993), 79–97; Beard (1994), 749–55; Kuttner (1995), 53–68; Galinsky (1996), 288–331.

[115] For the following points, see Weinstock (1971), 292–6; Beard (1994), 749–55; Kuttner (1995), 53–68.

Venus, had libations poured to them at meals along with the gods, or displayed themselves associating with gods on monumental statuary. Anyone celebrating a triumph or leading the *pompa circensis* was 'Jupiter for a day', clad in the god's robes and with his face painted red like the statue's. Nothing, then, comes from nothing, yet the status of an Augustus or a Nero was something new, in scale and in kind. Even the cult offered the emperor in the Greek East, for all its precedents in Hellenistic ruler-cult, is in sum 'a new phenomenon'.[116] In Rome, no human was the object of cult between Romulus/Quirinus and Julius Caesar; considering how much warrant for divinisation there was in the local and neighbouring cultures, it is testimony to the tenacity of the Republic's communal ideology that this apparently natural development was fended off for so long.

While the ideas of a continuum between Republic and Principate, and between human and divine, are clearly vital, the Romans were self-conscious about the innovatory nature of the new system – either in a spirit of pride (*deos enim reliquos accepimus, Caesares dedimus*, 'the other gods we have inherited from tradition, but the Caesars are our own contribution', Val. Max. *Pr.* 4), or outrage (*bella pares superis facient ciuilia diuos*, 'the civil wars will put the *diui* on a par with the gods above', Luc. 7.457). The new system was ambiguous and indeterminate in important respects, making it possible for the emperor's status as divine or human, revolutionary or traditional, to remain, in the last resort, uncategorisable.[117] This indeterminacy allowed for multiple responses and initiatives from all orders and areas of the Empire, accommodating the Emperor's unparalleled power while incorporating him into traditional frames. Once again, we see religion to be the Romans' most supple and responsive medium for experiment in the face of novel demands.

Until quite recently modern scholarship has been notoriously unsympathetic to the entire apparatus, falling with relief on texts such as Seneca's *Apocolocyntosis*, which appeared to give weight to the view that the educated regarded the business of apotheosis as a charade.[118] In fact, the existence of such parodic texts may just as well be taken to prove the

---

[116] Millar (1984), 53; cf. Price (1984), 54–9, and, in general, Versnel (1993), 218–19.

[117] Price (1984), 220, 233; cf. Elsner (1995), 167–72 for the divinity/humanity of the Prima Porta statue of Augustus. It was not for nothing that Varro grouped divinised humans in his category of *di incerti* (frr. 214–15).

[118] Price (1984), 11–19 and (1987), 87–91.

opposite: that the cult was a vigorous and muscular institution which could provoke and sustain interrogation and debate. The entitlement of a deceased emperor to apotheosis was never automatic, but had to be debated.[119] Just as 'le critique appartenait ... à la technique mythographique',[120] so criticism and testing was part of the apotheosis technique.

Such debate was the work of the elite. It is important to remember that it was also precisely the elite who were the main consumers and producers of the artefacts that did so much to mould attitudes to the new dispensation. At the beginning of the Principate, the elite were the ones who were most intimately affected by the religious revolution, who had to readjust the most, and whose opinion mattered most to Augustus.[121] For modern observers, who may perhaps instinctively see the divinisation of Augustus as a charade to impress the populace, it is salutary to remember that inventive reflection upon Augustus' divinity carried on in the elite forms of cameo and poetry even after such an important watershed as 28 BCE, when divine assimilation in the public mediums of coinage and state art was sharply curtailed.[122]

A prominent example of such inventive reflection may be found in Horace's *C.* 1.12, where the status of the *Princeps* is seen against the background of a systematic exploration and questioning of categories of divinity. The poem opens with the poet asking the Muse which man or hero or god she is going to celebrate (*Quem uirum aut heroa ... | ... sumis celebrare, Clio?|quem deum?*, 1–3). This impressive opening alludes directly to the opening of Pindar's second *Olympian*, where Pindar asks his lyre-commanding hymns 'What god, what hero, what man shall we celebrate?' Pindar answers his question immediately, with Zeus, Heracles, and Theron (3–7), but Horace does not begin to fill in the responses to his question until the fourth stanza, when he mentions Jupiter (without naming him). In Horace's Rome, the categories of god, hero, man are not what they were in Pindar's Greece; as the poem moves to its climactic evocation of Augustus as the one who straddles all three categories at once, it reveals the porosity of the divisions constructed by Greek and Roman traditions.

The first sign of the difficulty of keeping characters in the right

---

[119] Price (1987).   [120] Scheid (1993), 126.   [121] Kuttner (1995), 66.
[122] Galinsky (1996), 314; cf. Pollini (1990).

containers comes with the inherently transgressive Dionysus. Horace
has mentioned Jupiter first (13–18), and then the god who was born
directly from him, Pallas (19–21). He now turns to Liber (Dionysus),
who is in the same stanza as Diana / Artemis and Apollo (21–4). By this
grouping Liber is one of the Olympians, and Horace hereby activates a
problem of classification in Greek cult. Dionysus' status as one of the
twelve Olympians in Greece was fluctuating, for he oscillated in and out,
often alternating with Hestia.[123] In placing here a god whose status as a
true Olympian was problematic, Horace shows that the Greek categories
are not as tight as they might have appeared. In a Roman context, more
problems emerge, for Horace has here promoted Liber out of the category he occupies in Roman cult (and elsewhere in his own poetry). For
the Romans, Liber was one of the second category in Pindar's and
Horace's scheme, the heroes or demigods, such as Hercules and the
Dioscuri, who are mentioned together as a group in the next stanza
(25–8).

A gentle central stanza, describing the calming effects of the Dioscuri
upon storms at sea, mediates between the Greek and Roman halves of
the poem (29–32, the eighth of fifteen stanzas).[124] When we come into the
Roman half, the first name we meet is Romulus, the Roman counterpart
to the demigods who closed the Greek half (33): like them he is a twin,
the son of an immortal father and a mortal mother, who achieves
immortality thanks to his mighty services. But the Roman half of the
poem immediately reveals its arrangement to be based on different
criteria from those of the Greek first half. The Greek half was organised
around categories of divinity, presenting gods and then demi-gods (with
Dionysus bridging the two categories), and no men (apart from Or-
pheus, who is praised for two stanzas before Jupiter, 5–12). The Roman
half in a sense fills in the missing part of the triad, 'men',[125] but it is
important to see that this half is organised historically and chronologi-
cally, beginning and ending with individuals who cross the boundaries
(Romulus, Julius Caesar and Augustus). This portion of the poem opens
with a panoramic stanza that takes us from the foundation of the city in
war (Romulus) and peace (Numa, 33–4), to the end of the monarchy and
foundation of the Republic (Tarquin, 34–5), and finally to the end of the

---

[123] Burkert (1985), 125.   [124] West (1995), 58.   [125] Brown (1991), 328.

Republic with the noble death of Cato Uticensis (35–6).[126] After this survey of the sweep of history from which to choose, Horace gives us a parade of Republican worthies, who are all still men (37–44).[127] He does not return to any divinised human until after this parade, when, with *Iulium sidus* (47), he alludes simultaneously to the comet that marked the apotheosis of Julius Caesar and to the stellar status of his son, Augustus.

Caesar and Augustus, then, round off the Roman chronology, taking us back to Romulus, the first founder, and the only divinised Roman in history before them. The invocation of Jupiter which follows, and which closes the poem (49–60), rounds off the categories of divinity as well, by taking us back to the first praise of Zeus/Jupiter (13–18). The links between Jupiter and Augustus at the time of Horace's writing have been intensively studied;[128] Augustus is now not just a man who is the heir of Republican tradition, and not just a son of a god like Romulus, but one who enjoys a unique relationship (verging at times on identification) with the supreme god himself. Horace begins his poem by asking 'Which man, hero, or god to celebrate?', and gradually reveals that those categories are now such that one name can be the answer in each case.[129]

Such experiments are vitally important in constituting the new ideology. Indeed, at times Horace comes close to speaking openly about the role that poetry will have to play in constructing and guaranteeing the divinity of Augustus. In the first lyric collection, the closest he comes is a fantasy about some future performance in *C.* 3.25 (*quibus|antris egregii Caesaris audiar|aeternum meditans decus|stellis inserere et consilio Iouis?*, 'in what caves shall I be heard pondering over how to insert the eternal glory of Caesar amongst the stars and the council of Jupiter?',

[126] Brown (1991), 330.

[127] In a poem about the disruption of categories, Horace cannot resist tinkering with the divisions in this portion of the poem. Romulus, Numa and Tarquin belong together as kings, but what is Cato doing in their company (33–6)? If you believe Cato's Stoic philosophy, the wise man is better entitled to be called king than is Tarquin (Cic. *Fin.* 3.75); and the joke, if we may call it that, is reinforced by the name of the next person mentioned, the first of the Republican heroes, who is named 'little king' (*Regulum*, 37). Fabricius then disrupts Regulus' stanza, for Fabricius 'belongs to the group in the next stanza' (Nisbet-Hubbard (1970), 159).

[128] Feeney (1991), 220; add Pollini (1990) and Kuttner (1995), 34, 54–5.

[129] For discussion of other Horatian tactics for focusing on Augustus' ambiguous status between divine and human, see DuQuesnay (1995), 151, 181, 183, on *C.* 4.5.

3–6). Even in the fourth book of *Odes*, where he 'has poetry immortaliz-
ing the immortals', as Barchiesi puts it,[130] his list includes the familiar
demi-gods (Hercules, Dioscuri, Liber, 4.8.29–34), but not Augustus. In
his Epistle to Augustus, however, the interdependence of the poet and
the *Princeps* becomes a principal theme, as we see them locked together
in their ambitions of immortality. Augustus is superior to the usual
demi-gods, says Horace, for he is honoured during his lifetime as a god,
instead of having to wait until after his decease (*Ep.* 2.1.5–17).[131] The
phrase he uses for the demi-gods' apotheosis is an interestingly ambiguous one, capable of being read 'poetically', of the kind of elevation
depicted in epic and lyric, or else 'constitutionally', of the state's establishment of a cult: *deorum in templa recepti*, he says, 'received into the
temples of the gods' (6), where 'temples' may be the poets' 'regions of the
sky', or else the buildings of the city. When he comes to close the poem,
he returns to the issue of who controls access to these 'temples'. As he
introduces the section on the merits of various media to commemorate
such individuals as Alexander and Augustus, he describes the poets as
the *aeditui*, the 'temple-keepers', of the *uirtus* of the great (229–31). The
phrase is humble and self-deprecatory, as befits the genre,[132] but it reveals
Horace's awareness that it is he and Virgil and Varius (247) who will
eventually be in control of the *Princeps*' posthumous fate.

Power and immortality are the quintessential marks of ancient divinity, and the power and immortality of Augustus were both bound up
with the representations of poetry. The poets were vital participants in
the manifold debate about Augustus which conditioned the terms of his
power; when it came to immortality, the poets' role was even more
important, for they and Augustus knew that immortality was, in the end,
out of his hands.[133]

---

[130] Barchiesi (1996), 21; cf. 40–4, and Hardie (1993b), 134–5.
[131] See DuQuesnay (1995), 183 for the links with *C.* 4.5.
[132] Brink (1982), ad loc.
[133] Cf. Griffin (1984), 204.

CHAPTER

4

Ritual

The reality of ritual

Since 1902, when the first edition appeared of Wissowa's standard reference work, *Religion und Kultus der Römer*, cult has been at the centre of discussions of Roman religion.

Emphases have varied greatly over the years. In many earlier studies the focus on cult is perhaps rather grudging, as if the authors have regretfully come to the conclusion that they must concentrate on this, however repellent it may be, since there is after all nothing else which is native or authentic in Roman religious experience. An almost necessary corollary of such an approach to Roman ritual is an interest in origins at the expense of practice. The reality of ritual, according to this school, is to be found in its trace of an origin: meaningless and obsessive in its historical manifestation, at least Roman ritual holds up the promise of a recovery of a pristine, pure, and preferably rustic originary moment.[1]

Because the historically observable practice of Roman religion has in the last two generations come to be taken more seriously as the object of study in its own right, the interest in origins is correspondingly far more muted in recent scholarship; as Versnel puts it, '*origin* is not to be identified with *meaning*'.[2] The idea that the power or meaning of a rite is necessarily linked causally to its origin is, after all, as misplaced as the

---

[1] A sketch of this history in Beard (1987), 1–2.
[2] Versnel (1993), 242 (his italics); cf. 190, 218, 231, 233.

idea that the power or meaning of a myth or a word is linked causally to their origin.[3] Rather, the current emphasis is much more on the uses, the work, to which the word, myth, or rite is put (as we shall see, one of the kinds of work to which rite is put is to speculate on origins, but that work is not to be confused with the preservation of an historical trace). Recent analyses of Roman ritual have found that it was indeed doing a lot of work, if only on the level of the great amounts of time, money, and ingenuity that were lavished on ritual activity by the Roman elite.[4] From this more recent perspective as well, ritual may continue to be seen as the quintessentially Roman element of Roman religion, its real core.

Ritual has increasingly been regarded as powerfully real in other supposedly more substantive senses also – in the real world of politics and class hegemony, as the social cement for the Roman state, or as an ideological veil for the realities of power.[5] Much of the energy behind such approaches has come from the importance traditionally assigned to ritual by anthropology. The anthropological influence in Roman studies has been direct, but also indirect, mediated by the structuralist revolution in Greek studies: the impression was created that this was one area in which the techniques and successes of the Hellenists could be successfully transplanted.[6]

If revaluations of the significance of ritual have been a recurrent way of taking Roman religion seriously, they have also provided a life-line to those scholars who have wanted to take Roman literature seriously when it impinges on religion.[7] Here, too, it has appeared that the methodological gains of the Hellenists can be transferred, and here, too, it has appeared that the search for something socially powerful and real will be rewarded. Those portions of Roman literature which touch on ritual will be socially meaningful in ways that the rest are not. In public cult or domestic worship, and in their literary correlatives, surely we must unearth a genuine and authentic Roman religiosity, if such a thing exists.

The modern emphasis on ritual as the core of Roman religion and

---

[3] See Dennett (1995), 465 for a comprehensive attack, from a Darwinian perspective, on the 'genetic fallacy', 'the mistake of inferring current function or meaning from ancestral function or meaning'.

[4] Liebeschuetz (1979), 15–20; MacMullen (1981), 24–5, 129.

[5] Gordon (1990).   [6] E.g. Bremmer in Bremmer and Horsfall (1987).

[7] Habinek (1990); Cairns (1992a).

society is well grounded in copious ancient testimonia. Romans and Greeks alike regularly remark upon the pervasive power of religious practice at Rome.[8] What impressed Greek visitors like Polybius and Dionysius of Halicarnassus was clearly, in part, the sheer amount of cult activity they saw, both in public and private.[9] The scale and importance of Roman ritual activity is not in dispute. The problem is rather how to interpret all that activity, and especially, for our purposes, how to interpret the manifold literary texts which engage with it.

The unreality of ritual

We must acknowledge at the start that 'ritual', like 'myth', is a modern concept, which corresponds to no particular Roman or Greek word or concept.[10] Such observations are not always as devastating as they look, but in this particular case it matters a good deal that there was not a pre-existing subject out there, 'ritual', for Roman writers to address in the ways we wish they had. When Propertius writes about the cults of Bona Dea and Hercules at the Ara Maxima (4.9), juxtaposing a rite which excludes men and one which excludes women, he is irritatingly unforthcoming and imprecise about the cults' operations or significance, as Cairns remarks: 'It has long been observed that the Augustan poets' lack of pure intellectual curiosity, together with their literary inventiveness and their desire to emulate predecessors, led them, even when they probably knew Augustan Roman rituals and so forth first hand, to write not factual accounts of these events, but fantasy descriptions which are blends of the true facts and of Greek analogues and other models.'[11] Yet Propertius 'is not a colleague',[12] and the category of 'ritual' does not constitute a focus of enquiry for him as it does for us: he has his eye on gender and genre, and is making these cults and myths work within that frame.[13]

---

[8] Feeney (1991), 107.

[9] North (1976), 2, citing Polyb. 6.56.8 (public and private); Dion. Hal. *Ant. Rom.* 2.63.2 (more cult than anywhere in the world).

[10] Calame (1991); cf. Bell (1992), 219 against the idea of a universal category of 'ritual', and Sperber (1985), 26–9, making the same point about 'sacrifice'.

[11] Cairns (1992a), 67.

[12] To take over Nicole Loraux's dictum on Thucydides via Scheid's adaptation of it for Ovid: Scheid (1992), 118.   [13] DeBrohun (1994).

The Romans' objects of enquiry, then, were very different from ours. While some aspects of cultic behaviour were analysable (divination, for example, could be discussed by Cicero thanks to the fact that it had been discussed by Greek philosophers before him), entire fields of ritual activity were radically undertheorised, left practically undiscussed and unexamined by philosophers or historians. To moderns, sacrifice is a vital aspect of ritual, but, as Gordon points out, in the ancient world 'the system itself produced no theological account of the meaning and purpose of sacrifice'.[14] What there was instead, from the antiquarian tradition, was the accumulation and exegesis of multifarious cultic minutiae.[15] Whatever theorising went on about sacrifice was conducted in myth and poetry. And it goes without saying that poets were not concerned to elucidate the meaning of sacrifice exactly, but to put it to work in a system of meanings of another kind.

Further, we should question our instinctive assumption that ritual is fundamental, foundational, basic, an element of some potent earlier moment.[16] For ritual is not something underpinning or outside or before culture, but something enmeshed in culture's manifold forms. This is one of the reasons why it is so problematic to identify origins as the locus of ritual meaning: the hunt for the origin removes the ritual from the cultural context which makes it possible for it to be significant. The oblique influence from scholarship on Greek religion can be felt here in particular. If, in the search for meaning, students of Roman religion have traditionally looked to origins to find an earlier cultural moment, students of Greek religion have often looked in the same place to find a pre-cultural moment.[17] We may concur with Jonathan Z. Smith when he criticises scholars of sacrifice for 'the notion that here, in this religious phenomenon at least (or at last), is a dramatic encounter with an "other", the slaying of a beast . . . the notion that ritual – and therefore religion – is somehow grounded in "brute fact" rather than in the work and imagination and intellection of culture'.[18] Ritual is not an un-

---

[14] Gordon (1990), 206.

[15] Tresp (1914) on the Greek writers on cult; Rohde (1936) on the Roman.

[16] A major theme of Bell (1992); note esp. 37.

[17] E.g. Burkert (1979), 70: 'The problem remains, to find the underlying *unritualized* behavior' (my emphasis; my thanks to Polly Hoover for showing me the importance of this quotation, and in general for what I have learnt from her work in progress on sacrifice in Virgil and Lucan).   [18] Smith (1987), 197–8.

mediated encounter, then, or a trace of one, but already a representation, something which 'both *represents* and at the same time *constructs* an ideal reality', 'a meditation on one cultural process by means of another'.[19]

And it is a cultural process which negotiates in all kinds of creative ways between the real and the unreal, the expected and the unexpected. We have already seen in the previous chapter that the Romans were extremely adept at manipulating ritual in order to focus on what was real and unreal about their negotiations with divinity (above, pp. 95–6). Rather similarly, Elsner has investigated the studied way in which the 'point' of sacrifice is obscured in representations of the activity.[20] Roman sacrifice is directed to deity, but this goal is interestingly deferred: the encounter with divinity, the *tremendum*, is oddly off to the side, being looked at obliquely, so that the act of sacrifice and the person of the sacrificer are the focus.[21] The gods are the destination, but they are very seldom represented as participants or spectators,[22] and reliefs of sacrifice will as commonly show the doors of their temples closed as open. The effect is to block off any attempt to refer the action beyond the representation, to take it to its 'logical' conclusion.

Another way of making ritual fundamental is to see it as co-extensive with the cognitive system of a society, or at least as a code for the cognitive system of a society. Ritual, however, if it is a knowledge-system, is only one out of various knowledge-systems, and one we must be chary of assuming to be the most profound or foundational.[23] And it is a distinctly quirky kind of knowledge that ritual might be involved with, for it is very difficult to pin down quite what its object of knowledge is, or what the sense of a rite might be. The most radical position on the question of what it means to speak of 'the sense of a rite' is that of Staal (1989), who claims that ritual is inherently senseless, meaningless, performed for no goal or aim beyond itself. Even if we do not go that far we must be impressed by the great difficulty of talking about the meanings of ritual activity. As Scheid points out, 'understanding' a rite in Rome meant knowing how to perform it, and from this perspective the meaning or sense of the activity becomes an extremely problem-

[19] Seaford (1994), xii (original emphases); Smith (1987), 200.
[20] Elsner (1995), 198–9.   [21] Gordon (1990), 205.
[22] Gordon (1990), 205; a Hellenistic convention: van Straten (1993).
[23] Bloch (1989), esp. Ch. 1; cf. Sperber (1985), 46–8; Price (1984), 8–9.

atic concept.[24] If ritual is a language and means something to an audience, we must remember that the notional audience is the gods. They are the exegetes of the texts of ritual, and if the Arval Brethren, for example, did not understand the archaic Latin of their Hymn, then no doubt the gods did. The Romans distinguished clearly between the two communicative systems operating between humans and gods.[25] The gods send *auspicia* down to us, and we send *sacra* up to them; if we are the ones who interpret the *auspicia*, then they are the ones who can interpret the *sacra*.

The human observers of ritual will persist in trying to make sense of it, but the idea of 'the sense of a rite' is further complicated by the fact that in all societies – and Rome, as we shall shortly see, is no exception – the activity of making sense of ritual generates multiple interpretations amongst participants and observers: 'ritualized practices afford a great diversity of interpretation in exchange for little more than consent to the form of the activities'.[26] Indeed, ignorance and obscurity are part of the mystique and effectiveness of ritual.[27] We are always trying to home in on what ritual is really saying; but ritual is not really *saying* anything (except perhaps to the gods). It can only be made to say things, and too many things at that. Furthermore, the form of a ritual may remain constant over very long periods of time while generating or accepting entirely novel interpretations (this historical perspective is an essential corrective to the holistic views of ritual which are often a consequence of the anthropological snap-shot taken of a society at one moment in time).[28] Recent studies of such Roman rituals as the Lupercalia and the Parilia have revealed the way in which the accretion of new interpretations makes it possible for 'apparently static ritual forms . . . to continue to be meaningful when the society within which they are practised has radically changed'.[29] Ovid himself marks the discrepancy between the past circumstances which generated a form of action and the present maintenance of that form ('the form of what happened remains', *forma manet facti*, *Fast.* 2.379; 'but that custom still remains', *mos tamen ille*

---

[24] Scheid (1993), 116.

[25] Linderski (1982), 37; Kirk Freudenburg pointed out the importance of this distinction to me.   [26] Bell (1992), 186; cf. Sperber (1975), 8–22.

[27] Gordon (1990), 189; Hopkins (1991), 487–8.

[28] Bloch (1986), on the circumcision ritual of Madagascar.

[29] Beard (1987), 10; cf. Hopkins (1991); Wiseman (1995), 86.

manet, 6.414). At such moments the inherited actions of rite can appear at once frustratingly open and recalcitrant to interpretation.

As is shown by the powerful school of symbolic interpretation of ritual, people are always trying to find the 'real thing', the 'other thing', that ritual is mimetic of or congruent with. But this congruence is highly elusive, as Smith points out: 'ritual is not best understood as congruent with something else – a magical imitation of desired ends, a translation of emotions, a symbolic acting out of ideas, a dramatization of a text, or the like. Ritual gains force where incongruency is perceived and thought about.'[30]

These moments of incongruency are intensified in literary engagements with ritual: to adapt the terms of another of Smith's formulations, quoted above (p. 119), in literary representations of ritual we have yet another cultural process meditating upon the way in which another cultural process meditates upon another. And the kinds of meditation these cultural processes perform are very different. The 'meaning' or 'sense' of ritual is a most problematic concept, as we have just seen, yet literature is of course saturated with meaning and sense. The hermeneutics appropriate to the interpretation of each activity are very different – if, indeed, ritual is even susceptible to hermeneutics. Yet it is precisely the maddening recalcitrance of Roman ritual to hermeneutics that was no doubt in part responsible for the fact that it was covered over with exegesis, as the grain of sand is coated with pearl: as we shall see shortly, the two systems were in symbiosis, and the divorce we commonly make between ritual and its exegesis is open to serious question.

Poets who engage with ritual activity are very self-conscious about the refracted relationship between their work and its subject. In Chapter 1, we have already seen how self-conscious Horace's *Carmen saeculare* is about its oblique relationship to the rite of which it is so curious a part: let us now look at how a friend of Horace's meditates upon the relationship between rite and poetry.

Tibullus 2.1: space of ritual, space of poetry

The first poem of Tibullus' second book purports to be an enactment of a festival of purification, in which he will lead his *familia* around the

---

[30] Smith (1982), 63.

bounds of his farm to mark and guarantee the boundary between what is his and what is not.[31] The best-known such festival was that of the Ambarvalia (late May), and it is generally taken that this is the festival which Tibullus evokes.[32] As the creator of a poem which sets out to be mimetic of a ritual, Tibullus avails himself of the battery of resources which Callimachus had used to capture the strange reality of cult in his hymns.[33] In particular, we meet the same Callimachean use of vividly mimetic moments which are two-sided in their literary effect, at once conjuring up the absent reality and reminding us that the experience of reading the text is not the same as the experience of participating in the ritual. When the poem opens with the words 'Whoever is present' (*quisquis adest*), we know that we are not present; when Tibullus says 'Look!' (*cernite*, 15), we cannot see; and when he says 'Do you see the way that . . . ?' (*uiden ut . . .* , 25), we can only answer, 'Well, no'.[34]

Tibullus at once involves us in his representation and reminds us that it is just that, a representation. This carefully created sense of our distance from the reality of the performed rite helps to set up another kind of distance, the distance of the performance of the rite from reality. The poem is not only highly self-conscious about its own fictive nature, it is also highly self-conscious about the fictive nature of the rite which it is evoking. The powerful fictiveness of the rite comes from its insistence on the fact that this day is different, that its creation of a moment and area of security and tranquillity is a fantasy.[35] In cataloguing the perils and toils (ploughing, weaving, weeds, and wolves) which are to be suspended or warded off, the rite concentrates insistently on the incongruency (to use Smith's term) between the quotidian reality of those perils and toils and the ritual perfection that is so tightly circumscribed in time and space ('just today', 'just my farm'). In Tibullus' presentation the Ambarvalia becomes a tool for focusing on the discrepancies between what is actually the case in agricultural life and what is not. In this way his Ambarvalia uncannily fits the description of ritual given by Smith,

---

[31] My entire discussion of this poem is greatly indebted to Ross (1986); the excellence of his arguments makes it possible for me to be brief.

[32] Harmon (1986), 1943–55.

[33] Cairns (1979), 126–30; on Callimachus' techniques, Bing (1993) and Depew (1993), with Feeney (1993a), 238–40, on the two-sidedness of such authenticating techniques.   [34] Hunter (1992). 13 on Call. *Hymn* 2.4 ('Don't you see?').

[35] Ross (1986), 256–8.

according to whom '*ritual represents the creation of a controlled environ-ment* where the variables (i.e., the accidents) of ordinary life may be displaced *precisely* because they are felt to be so overwhelmingly present and powerful'.[36]

Tibullus is putting his reading of the Ambarvalia to extra work, however, for the real world of peril and toil which Tibullus is conjuring away is not straightforwardly the *real* world, but – as David Ross so compellingly shows – very largely the real world as mediated through Virgil's *Georgics*. More than one kind of lustration is going on here, in other words, for the rite of lustration marks off more than one space which is Tibullus' own. The world marked out by the rite, in which the threats of mundane agriculture and reality are delimited, looks at the world marked out by the poem, in which the threats of Virgil's authority are delimited as Tibullus circumscribes his own terrain of creativity. We may say that one of these acts of sequestration is more important or more real than the other, but in fact neither works to its full power without the other: their interaction mobilises all the associations of rustic ownership, self-sufficiency and creativity that have meant so much to Tibullus since the first poem of his first book.

The 'reality' of Ovid's Fasti

The most sustained poetic meditation upon Roman ritual is Ovid's *Fasti*. It may appear that, in sharp contrast to the fantasising nature of Tibul-lus' poetic and agrarian plots, Ovid's poem is dealing with the minutiae of genuine Roman practice, anchored in the solid ground of actual liturgy. Is not the *Fasti*, after all, a versification of the quintessentially practical and utilitarian state calendar itself?

Actually, it is not.[37] Ovid's poem is an amalgam of various religious, intellectual and poetical traditions. In particular, its relationship with the festal rhythms of the state, and with other calendrical records of those festal rhythms, is much more oblique and partial than is generally recognised. Of course, as Scheid puts it, 'Ovid utilizes as the thread of his work the model of the painted or carved calendars you could find in his

---

[36] Smith (1982), 63 (original emphasis). He continues: '*Ritual is a means of performing the way things ought to be in conscious tension to the way things are in such a way that this ritualized perfection is recollected in the ordinary, uncontrolled, course of things*' (original emphasis).   [37] Rüpke (1994).

day in public squares or in sanctuaries'.[38] But the first point we must take
stock of is that, as Scheid further argues, these painted or carved calendars were themselves by no means religious or cult documents in any
straightforward sense. They were memorials, without authority. They
alluded to, commented upon, and commemorated the mechanisms by
which state cult was regulated, but they were themselves not those
mechanisms.

Even their status as official, state documents is not secure. At the
origin of the calendar tradition which Ovid is following stands a most
remarkable document, an initiative which was the product of private
collaboration between a great Roman noble, M. Fulvius Nobilior, and
an entrepreneurial man of letters, Q. Ennius. Some 180 years before
Ovid began work on the *Fasti*, Fulvius adorned the walls of his new
temple of Hercules Musarum with lists of the Republic's consuls, and
with a painted twelve-month calendar. In a format which became canonical, Fulvius' calendar incorporated for the first time historical information (in particular the 'birthdays' of temples), together with scholarly
material such as an etymological discussion of the names of 'May' and
'June'.[39] The next significant innovation in the calendar tradition was the
work of Verrius Flaccus, a freedman *grammaticus* who was employed by
Augustus to instruct his grandsons (Suet. *Gram.* 17). This man set up an
inscribed calendar in the forum of Praeneste (the *Fasti Praenestini*,
which partially survives), and also published a (now lost) book on his
Fasti which must have been of major importance to Ovid in his own
work. To Fulvius' framework Verrius added a mass of new kinds of
material – such a welter of cult-information, etymologies and historical
aetiologies that the inscription takes on the trappings of scholarly commentary.[40] The siting of the scholar's inscribed Fasti interestingly illustrates its quirky and precarious status as a public document. The inscription was placed in the forum of Praeneste, at the centre of the city's
public life, but it was arranged in a semi-circle which acted as a focus for
the statue of Verrius Flaccus himself, placed opposite the monument
(Suet. *Gram.* 17). The architectural complex beautifies and in some sense

---

[38] Scheid (1992), 119.
[39] Macr. *Sat.* 1.12.16 for the etymologies (surely the work of Ennius). Important
   discussion of Fulvius' and Ennius' joint initiative in Rüpke (1995), 331–68; see
   Barchiesi (1994), 276–7 for Ovid's elision of these first *Fasti* at the close of his poem.
[40] Rüpke (1995), 120–1.

serves the state, but it simultaneously immortalises and exalts the freed-man scholar who created it, together with his skills and techniques.

The painted or carved monumental calendars, then, for all their imposing and apparently authoritative and practical character, had long had a multiply distanced relationship to the rites which they commented upon and commemorated. Indeed, their very topographical displace-ment is piquant in this regard as well, since a great many of the calendars were outside the city of Rome, so that their contents were remorselessly cataloguing cult activity which was actually taking place somewhere else.[41]

It is clear, then, that 'the relations between the written *fasti* and cult are not relations of total overlap'.[42] But students of Ovid's *Fasti* have to superimpose another layer of mediation before they can grapple with the cult, since the relations between Ovid's poem and the written *fasti* are not relations of total overlap either.[43] The poem's full title, *Libri Fas-torum*, signals this fact before we even begin the poem itself, for it means not 'Books *of* Fasti', but 'Books *about* Fasti'.[44] This incommensurability between Ovid's poem and the public calendars is not just a result of the fact that the poem is working off learned scholarship on the calendars as well as the (already learned) calendars themselves (a point that Ovid signals to us when he describes himself 'unrolling' *fasti, ter quater euolui signantes tempora fastos*, 1.657). Nor is it just a result of the fact that the poem is using all manner of antiquarian and religious learning in addi-tion, since Ovid could have used all this material and still stayed much closer to the format and boundaries of the *fasti*. Instead, he departs from and adds to the *fasti* in all kinds of ways. He adds in the 'movable feasts' of the *feriae conceptiuae*, for example. Again, he opens the work by means of a long and elaborate 'Callimachean' conversation with an inspirational and informative deity, Janus,[45] and then produces an osten-tatious declaration to alert us to the fact that we have not yet reached the supposed substratum to his work: 'On the other hand, as for what I have been allowed to learn *out of the Fasti themselves* . . . ' (*quod tamen ex ipsis licuit mihi discere fastis* . . . , 1.289–90).

---

[41] Beard (1991), 55; Price in BNP, Ch. 7. Note Rüpke (1995), 121, on how Verrius' *Fasti Praenestini*, most unusually, do have a reference to the local rite of Fortuna (10 April).　　[42] Scheid (1992), 121.

[43] Rüpke (1994) is fundamental here; cf. Phillips (1992), 65; Barchiesi (1994), 93–4.

[44] Rüpke (1994), 127–8.　　[45] Hardie (1991).

His most significant departure and addition, however, is announced prominently in the poem's first couplet:

Tempora cum causis Latium digesta per annum
    lapsaque sub terras ortaque signa canam.

I shall sing of times classified throughout the Latin year, along with their aetiologies, and also of the setting and rising of the stars.

Here the first line describes the traditional material of the Fulvian and Verrian fasti-format, whereas the second line announces a subject which is quite extraneous.[46] The recondite lore of Greek chronography, and the traditions of learned astronomical poetry (as practised by Aratus, Cicero, and the dedicatee Germanicus), are being annexed at this point for the first time to the fasti-tradition. Before the great Codex-Calendar of 354 CE, the Roman fasti-tradition practically never includes any astronomical or astrological information, and certainly not on the systematic scale which we observe in Ovid's poem.[47] Ovid's self-consciousness about his innovation is marked by an arch question which comes only six lines after the passage quoted in the previous paragraph, when he showed how the *fasti* 'proper' are only one element of his material. The question comes at the moment that he introduces his first astronomical notice, the setting of the Crab: *quid uetat et stellas, ut quaeque oriturque caditque, | dicere?* ('what is there to stop me telling of each star's rising and setting?', 1.295–6).

The result of this great act of originality is that Ovid commits himself to following, as Miller puts it, 'not one, but two temporal patterns, the rhythms of the sky as well as the regular round of celebrations in Rome'.[48] And since the material Ovid exploits for the astronomical side is all drawn from Greek astrology and mythography, with its multitude of catasterisms, we observe an important dichotomy being set up in the first two lines of the poem: to put it bluntly, one of his temporal patterns is Roman, and one is Greek.[49] These two patterns were, of course, being

---

[46] Rüpke (1994), 129; King (1994), 32–8; Newlands (1995), 27–30.

[47] Rüpke (1994), 129 and (1995), 154–5; cf. Miller (1991), 9 (who also points out how Ovid is trumping Propertius, who had promised in his 'aetia-book' to sing only of rites, dates, and names (*sacra diesque canam et cognomina prisca locorum*, 4.1.69)). It is very rare indeed to find such a mention as *Sol in Cancro* in the *Fasti Venusini* for 20 June (*CIL* 1,2.301).   [48] Miller (1991), 9.

[49] Important discussion in Newlands (1995), esp. Ch. 1.

harmonised by Augustus as Ovid wrote. Julius Caesar had first corre-
lated the solar year and the Roman civil year, but in 9 BCE Augustus had
to make definitive corrections. These corrections were memorialised in a
mighty complex on the Campus Martius: a massive captured Egyptian
obelisk acted as the gnomon for a meridian line, alongside which were
marked – in Greek letters – the zodiacal signs and phases of the natural
year as revealed by Greek science.[50] The whole complex 'thus specifically
commemorated Augustus' military and cultural control over the
Graeco-Roman world', and Ovid's bold decision to make his new genre
a dialogue between Greek and Roman temporal and ideological patterns
must be read in the light of Augustus' own dialogues between these
domains.[51]

The 'Greek' pentameter which supplements the very first hexameter of
the poem is a dramatic declaration of intent, announcing that Ovid's
treatment of Roman ritual will be in continual dialogue with another
form of knowledge and another frame of reference. What difference does
this make to our readings of Ovid's exegeses of ritual?

The exegeses of ritual

Sperber (1975) reorientated the study of ritual exegesis by insisting that
the native interpretation of ritual symbolism is part of the symbolic
system, not a spurious or dispensable addition to it. His insights were
exploited by Beard in her study of the religious meaning of the Roman
Fasti, in which she vindicated the ancient exegeses of the festivals as a
dynamic part of the larger cultural activity which we label 'Roman
religion'.[52] Ovid's poem, with its exegetical parameters flamboyantly
enlarged to include Greek myth and astral learning, is a challenge even
to Beard's more generous definition of ritual exegesis. We will try to
meet that challenge, but first we may chart the principal ways in which
Ovid's poem conforms to the 'rules' of Roman ritual exegesis.

One of the most striking aspects of Roman exegesis is its multiple
nature, particularly in aetiology, which is the focus of practically all

---

[50] So much is certain, even if the criticisms made of Buchner (1982) by Schütz (1990)
prove to be irrefutable.   [51] Newlands (1995), with the quotation from 24.
[52] Beard (1987); cf. Scheid (1992); Barchiesi (1994), 216.

exegesis.[53] This will have been a feature of Roman life even in archaic Rome. North is wholly correct to insist that from the very beginning of organised festival activity in Rome multiple interpretations must have been possible of any given rite.[54] Such manifold explanations are in part a result of the historical adaptability of cultic forms which we remarked upon above (p. 120). If new interpretations may supersede old ones over time, then at periods of transition, and even long after, we must expect to find variance. But there is more to multiple exegesis than development, for the competition of interpretations is endemic to the system. Modern readers may find this multiplicity baffling, for we tend to think of aetiology as bad history, a botched recovery of the past, although it is of course not that at all, but rather the ancients' way of doing theory. Modern readers may also find this openness to multiple interpretation baffling or ridiculous because they are influenced by the notion that a religion should be intent upon the propagation of a revealed truth, which cannot be multiplied without the risk of error or heresy. It is worth stressing, therefore, that the Roman religious tradition is by no means unique in being self-consciously open on the question of the interpretation of rites.

On 7 October, 1993, *The New York Times* gave a description of the Shinto ceremonial in which the priests periodically demolish the temple of the sun goddess Amaterasu, and then relocate the goddess – 'or at least the boxes containing an ancient mirror said to embody her spirit' – into a new temple a few yards away. This is a rite of great moment and great expense, costing 300 million dollars, yet its motivation remains opaque to the participants, and even to the priests. As we hear the journalist interrogating a senior Shinto priest, we are transported back to the pages of Ovid's *Fasti*:

> Why, every twenty years, does Japan rebuild its most sacred shrine, uprooting the sun goddess Amaterasu from her old sanctum and resettling her in a new one? 'I'm not really sure,' said Kenichi Yano, a senior priest at the shrine . . . 'There are many theories,' he said, from renewing the goddess's spirit to renewing the Japanese culture. 'But people have attached many different meanings to the twenty–year intervals, and we are not sure which of them are true.'

[53] Beard (1987); Harries (1989), 184; Miller (1992), 14–28; Fantham (forthcoming) on Ov. *Fast*. 4.783–806.   [54] North (1989), 603–4.

The Romans appear to have had a keener relish for such multiple exegesis than the Greeks. The difference has been explained in chronological terms: whereas the complex modern society of imperial Rome had to cope with a welter of opposing explanations for ritual, in the unitary and oral archaic Greek state everyone would have agreed on a single aetiology.[55] We may wonder whether such monolithic communitarianism was actually possible in archaic Greece;[56] still, even in the undeniably complex and modern Greece of the Roman Empire, the tendency is for less emphasis on multiple aetiology than in Rome. An instructive comparison presents itself in the form of two books Plutarch wrote on Roman and Greek aetiologies for current practices (almost all ritualistic). Whereas Plutarch's *Roman Questions* practically all have multiple aetia (86 out of 113), his *Greek Questions* very rarely do (3 out of 59), and even when Plutarch introduces a single 'answer' for a Roman 'question', he still introduces it with disjunctive ἤ ('or else' . . .). The Greek lore is presented as fossilised, the Roman as still in the process of formation.

Ovid reduplicates these cultural patterns, shunning multiple aetiologies for his Greek mythic material, and cultivating them for his Roman cultic material.[57] Ovid not only deploys many different aetiological explanations for various festivals and ritual practices; he also, crucially, deploys many different kinds of aetiological explanation at once. The studies of the Parilia (21 April) by Beard and Price bring out very clearly the self-conscious variety, even incompatibility, of the types of explanation offered.[58] After telling us how we should purify ourselves with water and then burn straw and jump over it as the climax of our observance of the rite, Ovid pauses (*Fast.* 4.783–4):

> expositus mos est; moris mihi restat origo:
> turba facit dubium coeptaque nostra tenet.

---

[55] E.g., Graf (1992).

[56] In late archaic Athens, aetiologies involving Theseus were grafted on to the festivals of the Pyanopsia and Oschophoria (Calame (1995), 189–201), so that there must have been a stage of transition during which the old versions were remembered as well; cf. Hall (1995) on the systematic transformations of aetiological myths about the Argive Heraion as the site changed hands; and Parke (1977), 156, 161–2 on the diverse aetiologies of the Attic festival of Skiraphoria.

[57] Newlands (1992), 51; cf. Hardie (1991), 63 and Barchiesi (1991), 8 on the difference between Ovid and Callimachus in the treatment of multiple aetiologies.

[58] Beard (1987); Price in BNP, Ch. 4; cf. Graf (1992).

The custom has been set out; the origin of the custom still remains for me to expound. The host of aetiologies makes me uncertain what to think and holds up my progress.

He proceeds to expound a series of seven possibilities, which range over the same modes of explanation as those exploited a century later by Plutarch in his *Roman Questions*, and which even use the same introductory phrasing (*an quia . . . ? an quod . . . ? an magis . . . ?*; 'or is it because . . . , or is it because . . . , or is it rather . . . ?', 787, 791, 799; compare Plutarch's frequent use of ἢ διότι . . .; ἢ διότι . . .; ἢ μᾶλλον . . .;).[59] The explanations come from 'natural science (fire as a natural purifier); philosophy (fire and water as opposing elements)'; Roman custom (practices of exile and marriage); 'Greek myths (Phaethon and Deucalion); accident (chance fire caused by shepherds); Roman myth (Aeneas and Troy)', and finally Roman history (the foundation of the city).[60]

There is indeed, as Beard puts it, 'a certain tension between the different styles of exegesis',[61] and it is a tension which many modern students of Roman cult have clearly found very frustrating, since the mass of incompatible alternatives distracts them from the indigenous and fundamental aspects of Roman cult, making them uncertain what to think and holding up their progress.[62] But rather than chastise Ovid for not having the same kind of unitary interest in authentic ritual as a modern scholar, we should concentrate on the intellectual work made possible by the incongruencies perceptible between all these different categories. The tension is very productive. This is the birthday of Rome, after all, the explanation which Ovid places in a culminating position, and elaborates with the story of the augury contest of the twins and the death of Remus (801–56). The foundation of the city is now viewed in a variety of interpretative contexts, for the day is multiply over-determined as a moment of origins of all kinds. The cosmogonic perspective we are given with the explanation of the warring primary elements (787–9) now enables us to read the beginning of the natural universe as

[59] Verrius Flaccus suggests himself as a common source: see Rose (1924), 35–43, for Plutarch's use of Flaccus.   [60] Price in BNP, Ch. 4.   [61] Beard (1987), 10.

[62] Latte (1960), 6 n.2. Rather, Fantham (forthcoming), Intro. III (i) (c), on the presence of Greek mythic aetiologies along with Roman historical ones: 'Far from being an obstacle, exegesis is Ovid's licence: the different conceptions of cause offer a glittering variety of treatments and themes.' Ovid then becomes a forerunner of Versnel (1990) and (1993).

the first link in a chain leading to the potent historical beginning moment
that is Rome – here Ovid acknowledges Virgil's fusing of cosmogony
and imperial aetiology.[63] The Trojan migration is inevitably the beginning of Roman national life (799–800), but even the new beginning of
human life in Greek myth (Deucalion, 793–4) may now be interpreted as
the beginning of Roman life. The fire and water of the ritual are the
foundation of biological, natural life itself (*uitae causa*, 791–2), marked
as such by the city's ceremonies of exile and marriage. The most Ovidian
touch, however, is the third to last possibility, that it was just an
accident, just a spark that happened to catch when shepherds were
carrying rocks (and even then it was the second spark . . . ; 795–8).
According to this explanation, the origin is quite random – and it is
random chance which creates the occasion for his narration of the city's
foundation (*ipse locum casus uati facit*, 807).

The power of the passage comes from the attempt to harmonise its
Roman totalising impetus (all explanations lead to Rome) with the
fragmented and contradictory atmosphere created by the competition of
frameworks (do a Greek cosmogony and a Greek myth *have* to lead to
Rome? Maybe it was all just an accident?). The incongruency between
the origin and the consequences is compelling, whichever origin and
whichever consequences we select.[64] The work which our perception of
this incongruency forces upon us is in our terms perhaps intellectual
rather than religious, but this is not a distinction that has currency for
Ovid.

Ovid's treatment of the Parilia, then, is the degree zero of ritual
interpretation: a massively over-determined sensation of originary
power, linked with the random and contingent.

Roman ritual in a Greek frame

The *Fasti*'s negotiation between Greek and Roman is an ancient feature
of Roman exegesis. From the first recorded Roman aetiologies of cult,
we see Roman scholars and poets making comparisons with Greek cults,
and making them the origins for Roman ones. In the second century BCE

---

[63] Hardie (1986).
[64] My reading of Ovid's aetiological interest is greatly indebted to Barchiesi (1994),
202–25; for the tension between totalising and fragmenting explanations, see
Hardie (1993a), esp. 1–3, on Virgil and his successors.

Accius describes the Cronia in Greece, and then explicitly says that the custom was taken over from there by the Romans for the Saturnalia.[65] Whereas both ancient and modern scholars have been able to confer prestige and significance on Roman ritual by focusing on its antique and indigenous aspects, the Roman aetiological tradition was able to add another technique – that of casting Roman ritual as Greek.

The interplay between these perspectives has been the subject of a number of important recent discussions.[66] The ongoing scholarly debate over this issue is testimony to the power of Ovid's framework, which continues to be a good tool for thinking about the issues with even in a culture unimaginable to the poet. One line of interpretation which I think we must view with scepticism is that which constructs a progress in the poem from Greek frivolity to Roman seriousness, in which the Greek element is superseded as we come closer to the core of what is genuinely Roman. Phillips has investigated Ovid's treatment of the Lemuria and Parentalia, the festivals of the dead, taking as his lead a definition of religion as that which 'integrate(s) "liminal" situations such as death and theodicy into prevailing societal "knowledge"'; Phillips concludes that Ovid 'emphasizes what he considers the ideological core of Roman religion in opposition both to Greek religion (Orion) and Augustus' tinkerings (genius cult). In his view, the answer to death lies in the historical stability of two festivals, in contrast to capricious Greek transformation or equally capricious Augustan introductions.'[67] Phillips' approach shows clearly the characteristic modern scholarly interest in restoring the quintessential nature of Roman cult, and is representative of a wide-spread frustration at the presence of alien material which smudges the patina of this quintessence. But we do not isolate the elements that make Roman religion a serious system by eliminating what we feel to be extraneous; rather, we see how serious the system could be by acknowledging its dynamic comprehensiveness.

Again, Parker asks whether it was the Roman or the Greek aetiologies for the Lupercalia which Ovid really believed or wants us really to believe (*Fast.* 2. 267–380).[68] But rather than taking sides we should observe the way in which the terms 'Roman' and 'Greek' are implicated

---

[65] Accius fr. 3 Courtney (1993).

[66] Fantham (1983); Harries (1989); Phillips (1992); Parker (1993); Barchiesi (1994), 203–7; especially now Newlands (1995).

[67] Phillips (1992), 65, 72; see Newlands (1995), 31.   [68] Parker (1993), 206–9.

in each other and define each other. Parker very successfully shows how various of Ovid's gods move from being 'either comic or criminal when they are in Greece' to being treated 'with complete respect in Italy' (216); but the point is that the very fashioning of this Roman seriousness needs the Greek as a screen upon which to project itself, and the screen is not dismantled after the showing.

The whole range of intellectual activity needed to compose and even begin to make sense of the *Fasti* is what religious and theological culture could be in Rome. The very elements that modern scholars may see as extraneous or inauthentic, such as the multiple aetiologies and the dialogue with the foreign, are precisely what make this intellectual activity possible. Throughout, Ovid is doing what Smith would have the historian of religion do, and that is engaging in '"defamiliarisation" – making the familiar seem strange *in order to enhance our perception of the familiar*. The success of any historian of religion's work depends upon a judgment as to whether this enhancement has taken place.'[69] By this criterion Ovid is a very considerable historian of religion.

Nostalgia ancient and modern

In the face, then, of our modern nostalgia for the originally and fundamentally Roman aspects of ritual, it is important to reassert the luxuriant intellectual and cultural power of Roman ritual exegesis. It is, however, likewise important to acknowledge the tremendous force which that nostalgia already commanded amongst the Romans themselves, who invented it, as one half of their ceaseless dialogue with modernism. In many Roman authors this nostalgia for a lost religious simplicity and authenticity is located in the past; it may also be located off to the side in the present, when it is often displaced into the country. Rustic past and present, after all, fuse in Roman moralising, as North points out: 'Elite accounts . . . exploit the idea of country life and of its religiosity in the interests of a moralising discourse associating the moral, the past and the rustic.'[70] The clearest example of such attitudes is to be found in Virgil's *Georgics*,[71] but the nexus is ubiquitous, and may be traced back at least to Cato's *De agricultura*.

---

[69] Smith (1982), xiii (original emphasis).   [70] North (1995), 142.
[71] E.g. 1.338–50.

Individual exploitations of this nexus of ideas vary greatly. Horace is perhaps more interested than anyone else in the nuanced relationship that exists between the city and the country, and his presentation of urban and rustic ritual therefore reveals a keen interest in the divisions and continuities that may be constructed within these categories. He certainly presents numerous images of rustic piety (*C.* 1.4; 3.8, 13, 18, 22, 23), but he 'anticipates' modern scholarship in concentrating on the dynamic interrelationship between public and private cult, and urban and rustic cult.[72] *C.* 3.22, for example, a two-stanza poem addressed to Diana as Horace plants a pine by his villa and sacrifices a pig, has been shown by Cairns to be not solely the act of private and rustic piety it may appear to be. The poem and the sacrifice are linked by the calendar to public cult in the city, for 13 August was not simply the day of Diana's festival throughout Italy, on which the reader assumes Horace's sacrifice to take place, but also the birthday of her temple on the Aventine Hill in Rome.[73] Henderson has taken the calendrical links with public ideology further, reminding us that this day was also the first day of Augustus' triple triumph in 29 BCE, and the day that Virgil's hero Aeneas spent in Evander's hut on the Palatine Hill, where later was to rise the temple-palace complex of Augustus and the siblings Diana and Apollo.[74]

In Henderson's words, Horace invites us to 'see *at once* the hierarchic division between . . . "public rites" . . . and "private rites . . . " – *and* the metonymic linkage in their sliding scale'; as he says, 'a person's prayer and ritual ought not to be *confused* with priestly state liturgy . . . ; but it followed in its wake, conditioned as a *widow's mite* simulacrum or cameo'.[75] Henderson's '*widow's mite*' refers to the following poem (*C.* 3.23), where Horace addresses a rustic lady (*rustica Phidyle*), assuring her that her sacrifice, however humble, has a role to play in the larger context of Roman religion. Her offerings to the Lares of incense, corn, or a pig (3–4), or even of nothing more than meal and salt (20), appease the Lares and ward off natural threats to her domain's fertility (5–8), even

---

[72] On the interpenetration of private/public, see above, pp. 5–6.

[73] Cairns (1982), 236–7.

[74] Henderson (1995), 136–7; cf. 113 for the synecdoche between Horace's 'private' sacrifice and the 'public' cult of Diana on the Palatine, celebrated elsewhere by Horace (C. 1.21).

[75] Henderson (1995), 112–13 (original emphases), with 'public rites' and 'private rites' a quotation from Festus 284L.

though her offerings are far inferior to the mighty beasts of the city's pontifical ritual, whose rearing in the Alban hills is beautifully evoked in the poem's central stanza (9–11). Once again, Cairns has demonstrated the linkages between Phidyle's ritual and the city's: 1 May is the occasion of an offering by women to the Lares and Penates for the safety of the crops, and also for the urban celebration by women of the festival of Bona Dea.[76] Further, the grand offerings of the state's *pontifices* provide a vast backdrop to the tiny offerings of the backwoods woman: the two patterns of sacrifice are part of an enormous and self-reinforcing continuum.[77]

Tibullus makes the theme of rustic piety peculiarly his own. He is capable of glancing at the kind of interrelationship between rustic and urban that we have seen in Horace;[78] but in general he concentrates on systematically grouping together many varieties of fantasy displacement. The first poem of his collection is a prayer for an idyllic rustic and religious existence, in which he forswears other forms of experience together with their forms of poetic expression;[79] as we have seen, this wish is powerfully reanimated within a ritual frame when he begins his second book. This idyllic existence is tied to numerous types of idealised life: linked with the lost Golden Age, either of humanity in general (1.3.35–50) or of his own idyllic childhood (1.10.15–26); associated with the pure piety of the female (1.5.27–8); always, projected as the hoped-for result of a relationship with the rustic deities (1.1.9–24 is the programmatic utterance).

As North (1995) so clearly demonstrates, such poetic images have acquired talismanic status in modern discussions of Roman religion, and have been internalised so thoroughly that it is difficult for us to realise how fundamentally they condition our assumptions about the historical development of Roman religion and the religious priorities of Romans of the late Republic or Empire. It is crucial to recognise that the Romans' nostalgia for rustic or private piety is not a natural reflection of a really existing phenomenon, but one element of a highly complex and self-conscious cultural debate. Again, it is Tibullus who most clearly displays this self-consciousness. After his conjuring of a rural idyll in his first poem, he returns to lament its loss in 1.5. Delia has spurned him for

---

[76] Cairns (1977), 538–40.   [77] Cairns (1977), 538–9.

[78] Cairns (1979), 130, on the links between the rustic and civic celebration of the Ambarvalia in 2.1.   [79] Elder (1962), 70–1; Lee (1974).

another, and he recalls the fantasy he had spun before this disaster: 'but I
fantasised a blessed life for myself', he says (*at mihi felicem uitam . . .
|fingebam*, 19–20), as he introduces a reverie of rustic felicity (21–34),
with a Delia learned in rustic rites (27–8). Now this dream is exposed as
the dream it always was, and he rounds off the memory with a recapitulation of the words that introduced it: 'that was my fantasy/fiction' (*haec
mihi fingebam*, 35).

The nostalgia for a pristine and secure private rustic piety is one that
Tibullus was already cultivating two thousand years before Kurt Latte.
The difference is that Tibullus knew it was a fiction.

Epilogue: knowledge

The problem of knowledge belongs at the end, not the beginning, of our enquiry. This is partly because the problem of their knowledge and ours provides the best context for drawing the threads of the argument together. More importantly, however, this placement reminds us that 'knowledge' does not represent an inert base of data as a starting-point, but is a dynamic issue in its own right. Knowledge about religion in Rome is not simply a matter of information: the definition of what will count as serious knowledge, and the control of access to those forms of knowledge, are inextricable elements of any society's self-fashioning and web of power.[1] Much of Roman political history, for example, may be read as a struggle over who is going to be allowed access to the knowledge necessary to mediate between gods and humans. Further, new forms of analysis or presentation of religious knowledge were constantly being imposed upon the 'matter', bringing with them new configurations and conflicts. The literature we have been discussing throughout the book is another form of knowledge, and, in the end, literature about religion is another form of religious knowledge: it is another set of possibilities, another distinctive series of interventions into the huge terrain of what could be thought and said and done about religion in the Roman world.

---

[1] Such is Foucault's contribution: Rouse (1994) is a suggestive introduction to Foucault's views on 'Power/Knowledge'; see Barton (1994) for a classicist's exploitation, and Wallace-Hadrill (1988) for a discussion of the social role of knowledge in Rome. One eagerly awaits A. Schiesaro's work in progress on 'The Boundaries of Knowledge in Latin Poetry'.

The problem of religious knowledge is difficult at every level. What, for example, did a Roman know of his religion, and how did he come to know it? These questions were exercising Momigliano in some of his last essays.[2] The religion of the city and the empire was vast in bulk, the product of centuries of unsystematic accretion; there were no authoritative master-texts, and no single body charged with oversight of the manifold rites. Many of the written documents which scholars have regarded as the bedrock of a system of knowledge turn out not to be such at all: the books of the priestly colleges, for example, were not sources of discursive information but records of practice.[3] Similarly, the mass of written material cluttering shrines and temples was not there to instruct, exactly, but to impress, commemorate, mystify and intimidate.[4] Of course it was possible to pick up pieces of information about deities and cults as an observer: there were spectacles of procession, theatre, dance and hymn in every city, and everywhere there were self-appointed experts to interrogate about the cults.[5] Yet none of this activity amounted to an education or training in religion, as Ovid makes clear for us in the *Fasti*, where one of his main themes is precisely how difficult it is to find out anything about Roman cult.[6]

For the practice of religion this lack of systematic inculcation of knowledge was irrelevant. Much of what a Roman 'knew' about religion was 'performative knowledge', requiring no 'theoretical justification', instilled in the course of the innumerable domestic and civic ceremonies which the citizen would have endured or enjoyed by the time he reached adulthood.[7] Especially in the light of the Christian tradition, with its catechisms, creeds and articles of faith, it is often difficult for modern observers to grasp how easily a religion may maintain itself in an environment where most of its practitioners are genuinely ignorant

---

[2] Momigliano (1987), 85–6, 163, 166. As he says, it is exceedingly difficult to find any references to instruction in religious behaviour. To his few citations I can add only a passage in Statius' *Silvae* (5.3.180–4), where Statius speaks of the many rites which his father taught his schoolboys, including the future emperor Domitian; but this presumably refers to exegesis of the kind practised by Plutarch or Ovid rather than to any 'instruction' in ritual.   [3] Scheid (1992), 122 and (1994).

[4] Gordon (1990), 184–91; Beard (1991).   [5] MacMullen (1981), esp. 14–34.

[6] Newlands (1992), 51.

[7] Quoted phrases from Balagangadhara (1994), 486, in his discussion of Roman *traditio* and its similarity to Hinduism; cf. Scheid (1990), 673–6, for the learning of ritual practice by the Roman citizen.

about practically everything outside the realm of performative knowledge. Yet modern Japan presents precisely this picture, as is shown by Reader (1991), in particular with his discussion of a survey carried out by the Soto Zen Buddhist sect, 'one of the largest and oldest Buddhist organisations in Japan': 'The survey in general showed a woeful lack of knowledge amongst members as to teachings, doctrines and facts about the sect, yet at the same time it showed extremely high levels of participation in memorial rites for the dead and various yearly rituals concerned with the dead that were carried out under its aegis.'[8] Even Christianity's rigorous educational system may not succeed in communicating more than performative knowledge, as Dr Johnson pointed out in a comparison with non-Christian religions: 'What account of their religion can you suppose to be learnt from savages? Only consider, Sir, our own state: our religion is in a book; we have an order of men whose duty it is to teach it; we have one day in the week set apart for it, and this is in general pretty well observed: yet ask the first ten gross men you meet, and hear what they can tell of their religion.'[9]

Beside such 'performative' knowledge, however, we must place systematising expositions of religious knowledge, which represent a different form of behaviour altogether. In the late Republic and early Empire such expositions blossomed, as part of the period's explosion of intellectual activity, resulting in a mass of material on augury, extispicy, astrology, on thunder-interpretation, priesthoods, and divinities.[10] The traditionally vital importance of religion to the elite is clearly shown by the fact that theology was one of the areas of Greek learning that they embraced with zeal, rather than leaving it to Greek practitioners along with geometry, arithmetic, astronomy and music.[11] Religious knowledge had always been the prerogative of the citizenry's elite; now, with a new aristocracy emerging from the hugely expanded citizenry of Italy after the Social War, there was a new market for these prestigious appurtenances of citizenship, together with a new and larger stage for those possessed of such knowledge to parade upon.

These new systems of knowledge were not helpful transcriptions of

---

[8] Reader (1991), 3–4. Such findings are powerful corroboration of Gordon's warning against 'too readily assuming that because it was "their religion" the Romans necessarily understood it': Gordon (1990), 189. [9] Chapman (1970), 751.

[10] Rawson (1985), 298–316; Beard (1994), 755–9.

[11] Wallace-Hadrill (1988), 227, 233.

fact but interventions with their own priorities and strategies. It is notorious that even a well-informed member of the Roman religious public such as Cicero could come away from reading Varro's *Antiquitates rerum humanarum et diuinarum* with the impression that he had up till then been wandering around like an ignorant stranger in his own city (*Acad. Post.* 1.9). Varro's system of religious knowledge was not an exposition in accessible or condensed form of what his peers knew latently anyway, any more than was his system of linguistic or civic knowledge. Varro's categories of arrangement ('people, places, periods and things') enabled him to dominate any body of knowledge,[12] and it was this form of mastery that made him able to speak with expertise and authority. After all, he said that even the Greek priests of the mysteries of Samothrace did not know what he knew about their cult: he was going to write them a letter to put them right (fr. 206).

Cicero's reaction to Varro's work helps us to see that there was no one Roman religious system existing essentially, inherently meaningful, waiting to be participated in. Rather, what we call 'Roman religion' or the 'Roman religious system' was compounded of all kinds of different forms of religious knowledge, from the performative to the philosophical, literary or antiquarian. The 'system' was not a defined entity: even its boundaries were very unsystematically policed, as emerges from Phillips' study of sanctions on magical practices.[13] The structuralist model which informs so much cultural anthropology often proceeds as if a society does have an immanent collective system of cognition underpinning its religion; yet such an approach does not do justice to the competitive variety of knowledge systems in any society, and ends up confusing the patterns constructed by the outside observer with the actual thought of the participants.[14] Any attempt to make sense of religious activity must take place within a particular knowledge system, which will condition the kind of sense that will emerge. This is true of the Romans, and it is true of us observing the Romans. The activity of making sense by making connections is one that happens contingently at the moment of observation and participation (whether ancient or modern): this is the moment, then or now, at which Roman religion is apprehended as a system. There may be very little overlap between our systems of Roman

[12] Horsfall (1982), 287.   [13] Phillips (1991b).
[14] Such are the criticisms of traditional cultural anthropology made by Bloch (1989): see esp. 106–36, 152–65.

religion and theirs, but the lack of overlap is what makes interpretation happen. Just as, within their systems, meaning was generated in the interaction between the various genres of belief, so too for us, as observers, meaning is generated in the attempt to close the gaps between their systems and ours.[15]

The Romans' system, or system of systems, satisfied for a millennium the bewilderingly various requirements of a uniquely successful society. From the third century BCE, part of this creative and dynamic system was an ever-evolving literary tradition, 'original, self-assured and aggressive' from the start,[16] which produced works of very great beauty, power and intelligence. These works were not beautiful, powerful or intelligent inasmuch as they reflected or mirrored other religious discourses, but by virtue of the fact that in their interaction with other discourses they were doing irreplaceably challenging cultural work of their own. We should, therefore, use the word 'context' with care. It is important to move away from formalism by placing Roman literature within its intellectual, social and political contexts. But in so doing we must beware of making those other contexts 'primary' and 'real', with literature 'secondary' and 'unreal'; for literature is itself, so to speak, another context, another set of discourses with distinctive capacities.[17]

We have repeatedly seen how self-conscious Roman literature was about the fact that it was not tautologous, a mimicry of other discourses. As moderns with a nostalgia for genuine experience, we may wish that Roman literature had been more 'faithful' to 'real' religion, but this is to overlook the fact that there was no one real religion for literature to be faithful to in the first place. Further, the wish to make Roman literature track other supposedly more real practices derogates drastically from the important cultural work which literature was enabled to do by virtue of its own characteristic power. The cultic atmosphere of Virgil's *Aeneid* is an instructive example. Although there are many evocations of

---

[15] Cf. Iser (1978), 166–9, on the fact that 'it is the gaps, the fundamental asymmetry between text and reader, that give rise to communication in the reading process' (167); further on this theme, Kennedy (1993), Ch. 1, and Feeney (1995), esp. 311–12.   [16] Momigliano (1975), 17.

[17] Cf. Wheeler (1993), 240, arguing against those forms of new historicism that 'dissolve literature back into its historical complex, reasserting . . . a primacy for history of which literature is the secondary reflection'; cf. Kramer (1989), 114–15; Kennedy (1993), 7–8.

Roman cult throughout the poem, Virgil is less concerned with accurate and minute points of detail than one might have expected.[18] The poem's prayers, in particular, are homerically 'literary' in their phrasing, markedly less cultic or technical even than the prayers in Ennius' *Annales*.[19] Virgil is not interested in reproducing documentary evidence of what Roman priests said; he is, even, not as interested as we might want him to be in creating a specifically Roman atmosphere at such moments.[20] He is interested in making the Homeric experience part of the Roman experience. Why this should be a less significant cultural project I fail to understand.

The common instinctive dismissal of Roman religious literature as marginal or 'only literary' misses the point: the variety of written texts, the explosion of knowledge of all forms, had changed the whole set of imaginative and intellectual possibilities. This transformation is most evident in the context of the Augustan revolution, as Liebeschuetz well points out: 'It may well be that the most important long-term effect of the Augustan revival was literary, a reshaping of the religious imagination of the Romans as a result of the religious colouring of Roman literature.'[21] Yet literature will have been an actively moulding force from the beginning. The crusty old senator who sees Plautus' *Amphitryo* or hears a reading of Ennius' *Euhemerus* at a friend's house may say 'that is not my way, or our way', but in so doing he is engaging with these novelties: they are now part of his way, if only as negative definition.

If the Romans' knowledge of their religion was partial, ours is inescapably even more so. We have lost so much of what made up their religious world, yet even what remains is overpowering in its bulk. My aim in this book has been a limited one, to argue that we should adopt a less patronising attitude towards the great body of religious knowledge that does, fortuitously, survive, in the form of Roman literature. Even so, I have repeatedly found myself in the position of Cicero after reading Varro's *Antiquitates*, startled into realising that the apparent process of

---

[18] Horsfall (1991), 43, 138.   [19] Hickson (1993), 27–31, 141–4.

[20] Although I have criticised Silius Italicus for 'his failure to evoke the potency of Rome's antique cult and ritual' (Feeney (1991), 311), I should have seen that he had understood very clearly Virgil's procedure, and wanted to create a Virgilian, rather than a Livian, mode of representing ritual, even if it was historically Roman ritual.

[21] Liebeschuetz (1979), 89; cf. Momigliano (1987), 62, 72.

acquiring knowledge is in fact primarily a process of realising the extent of one's ignorance. In the end, as usual, Dr Johnson was right: 'Why, Sir, we know very little about the Romans.'[22]

[22] Chapman (1970), 464.

Bibliography

Alvar, J. (1985) 'Matériaux pour l'étude de la formule *sive deus, sive dea*', *Numen* 32: 236–73

Asad, T. (1993) *Genealogies of Religion: Discipline and Reasons of Power in Christianity and Islam*. Baltimore and London

Axtell, H.L. (1907) *The Deification of Abstract Ideas in Roman Literature and Inscriptions*. Chicago

Badian, E. (1966) 'The early historians', in T.A. Dorey (ed.), *Latin Historians*, 1–38. London

Bakhtin, M.M. (1968) *Rabelais and his World*, trans. H. Iswolsky. Cambridge, Mass.
(1981) *The Dialogic Imagination: Four Essays*, ed. M. Holquist, trans. C. Emerson and M. Holquist. Austin

Bakker, J.T. (1994) *Living and Working with the Gods: Studies of Evidence for Private Religion and its Material Environment in the City of Ostia (100–500 AD)*. Amsterdam

Balagangadhara, S.N. (1994) *'The Heathen in His Blindness': Asia, the West and the Dynamic of Religion*. Leiden

Barchiesi, A. (1991) 'Discordant Muses', *PCPhS* 37: 1–21
(1994) *Il poeta e il principe. Ovidio e il discorso augusteo*. Rome
(1996) 'Poetry, praise and patronage: Simonides in Book 4 of Horace's *Odes*', *CA* 15: 5–47

Barchiesi, M. (1962) *Nevio epico*. Padua

Barton, T.S. (1994) *Power and Knowledge: Astrology, Physiognomics, and Medicine under the Roman Empire*. Ann Arbor

Beard, M. (1986) 'Cicero and divination: the formation of a Latin discourse', *JRS* 76: 33–46
(1987) 'A complex of times: no more sheep on Romulus' birthday', *PCPhS* 33: 1–15
(1989) 'Acca Larentia gains a son: myths and priesthoods at Rome', in M.M. Mackenzie and C. Roueché (eds.), *Images of Authority: Papers presented to Joyce Reynolds on the occasion of her 70th birthday*, 41–61. Cambridge
(1990) 'Priesthood in the Roman Republic', in M. Beard and J. North (eds.), 17–48
(1991) 'Writing and religion: *Ancient Literacy* and the function of the written word

in Roman religion', in J.H. Humphrey (ed.), *Literacy in the Roman World*, 35–58. Ann Arbor

(1993) 'Looking (harder) for Roman myth: Dumézil, declamation and the problems of definition', in F. Graf (1993a) (ed.), 44–64

(1994) 'Religion', in *CAH* IX, 2nd edn, 729–68

(1995) 'Re-reading (Vestal) virginity', in R. Hawley and B. Levick (eds.), *Women in Antiquity: New Assessments*, 166–77. London

(1996) 'Le mythe (grec) à Rome: Hercule aux bains', in S. Georgoudi and J.-P. Vernant (eds.), *Mythes au figuré*. Paris

Beard, M. and Crawford, M. (1985) *Rome in the Late Republic: Problems and Interpretations*. London

Beard, M. and North, J. (1990) (eds.) *Pagan Priests: Religion and Power in the Ancient World*. Ithaca

Beard, M., North, J. and Price, S.R.F. (forthcoming) *Religions of Rome*. 2 vols., Cambridge

Bell, C. (1992) *Ritual Theory, Ritual Practice*. Oxford

Bing, P. (1988) *The Well-Read Muse: Present and Past in Callimachus and the Hellenistic Poets*. Göttingen

(1993) 'Impersonation of voice in Callimachus' *Hymn to Apollo*', *TAPhA* 123: 181–98

Bloch, M. (1986) *From Blessing to Violence: History and Ideology in the Circumcision Ritual of the Merina of Madagascar*. Cambridge

(1989) *Ritual, History and Power: Selected Papers in Anthropology*. London

Bloch, R. (1963) *Les Prodiges dans l'antiquité classique: Grèce, Étrurie et Rome*. Paris

Blumenberg, H. (1985) *Work on Myth*, trans. R.M. Wallace. Cambridge, Mass. and London

Boardman, J. (1994) *The Diffusion of Classical Art in Antiquity*. Princeton

Bourgeaud, P. (1993) 'Quelques remarques sur la mythologie divine à Rome, à propos de Denys d'Halicarnasse (*ant. Rom.* 2, 18–20)', in F. Graf (1993a) (ed.), 175–87

Bowie, E.L. (1993) 'Lies, fiction and slander in early Greek poetry', in C. Gill and T.P. Wiseman (eds.), 1–37

Bremer, J.M. (1981) 'Greek hymns', in H.S. Versnel (ed.), *Faith, Hope and Worship: Aspects of Religious Mentality in the Ancient World*, 193–215. Leiden

Bremmer, J. (1987) (ed.) *Interpretations of Greek Mythology*. London

Bremmer, J. and Horsfall, N. (1987) *Roman Myth and Mythography*. London

Brillante, C. (1990) 'History and the historical interpretation of myth', in L. Edmunds (ed.), 93–138

Brink, C.O. (1982) *Horace on Poetry: Epistles Book II*. Cambridge

Brouwer, H.H.J. (1989) *Bona Dea: The Sources and a Description of the Cult*. Leiden

Brown, R.D. (1991) '*Catonis nobile letum* and the list of Romans in Horace *Odes* 1.12', *Phoenix* 45: 326–40

Bruit Zaidman, L. and Schmitt Pantel, P. (1992) *Religion in the Ancient Greek City*, trans. P. Cartledge. Cambridge

Buchner, E. (1982) *Die Sonnenuhr des Augustus*. Mainz

Bulloch, A.W. (1985) (ed.) *Callimachus: The Fifth Hymn*. Cambridge

Bulloch, A.W., Gruen, E.S., Long, A.A., and Stewart, A. (1993) (eds.) *Images and Ideologies: Self-Definition in the Hellenistic World.* Berkeley and Los Angeles

Burkert, W. (1979) *Structure and History in Greek Mythology and Ritual.* Berkeley and Los Angeles

(1985) *Greek Religion: Archaic and Classical*, tr. J. Raffan. Oxford

(1987) 'Oriental and Greek mythology: the meeting of parallels', in J. Bremmer (ed.), 10–40

(1992) *The Orientalizing Revolution: Near Eastern Influence on Greek Culture in the Early Archaic Age*, tr. W. Burkert and M.E. Pinder. Cambridge, Mass.

(1993) 'Mythos – Begriff, Struktur, Funktion', in F. Graf (1993a) (ed.), 9–24

Burnett, A.P. (1983) *Three Archaic Poets: Archilochus, Alcaeus, Sappho.* London

Buxton, R. (1994) *Imaginary Greece: The Contexts of Mythology.* Cambridge

Cairns, F. (1977) 'Horace, *Odes*, III, 13 and III, 23', *AC* 46: 523–43

(1979) *Tibullus: A Hellenistic Poet at Rome.* Cambridge

(1982) 'Horace *Odes* 3, 22: Genre and sources', *Philologus* 126: 227–46

(1984) 'Propertius and the battle of Actium (4.6)', in T. Woodman and D. West (eds.), *Poetry and Politics in the Age of Augustus*, 129–68. Cambridge

(1992a) 'Propertius 4.9: "*Hercules Exclusus*" and the dimensions of genre', in K. Galinsky (1992) (ed.), 65–95

(1992b) 'Theocritus, *Idyll* 26', *PCPhS* 38: 1–38

Calame, C. (1991) '"Mythe" et "rite" en Grèce: des catégories indigènes?', *Kernos* 4: 179–204

(1995) *The Craft of Poetic Speech in Ancient Greece*, trans. J. Orion. Ithaca and London

Cameron, A. (1995) *Callimachus and his Critics.* Princeton

Campbell, D.A. (1983) *The Golden Lyre: The Themes of the Greek Lyric Poets.* London

Cardauns, B. (1976) *M. Terentius Varro: Antiquitates Rerum Diuinarum.* Wiesbaden

Carpenter, T.H. and Faraone, C.A. (1993) (eds.) *Masks of Dionysus.* Ithaca and London

Catalano, P. (1978) 'Aspetti spaziali del sistema giuridico-religioso romano. Mundus, templum, urbs, ager, Latium, Italia', *ANRW* 2.16.1: 440–553

Chapman, R.W. (1970) (ed.) *Boswell's Life of Johnson.* Oxford

Clay, D. (1983) *Lucretius and Epicurus.* Ithaca and London

Clifford, J. (1988) *The Predicament of Culture: Twentieth-Century Ethnography, Literature, and Art.* Cambridge, Mass.

Coarelli, F. (1983) *Il Foro Romano. I. Periodo Arcaico.* Rome

Conte, G.B. (1994) *Genres and Readers: Lucretius, Love Elegy, Pliny's Encyclopedia*, trans. G.W. Most. Baltimore and London

Cornell, T.J. (1978) review of Wardman (1976), *CR* 28: 110–12

(1995) *The Beginnings of Rome: Italy and Rome from the Bronze Age to the Punic Wars.* London

Courtney, E. (1993) *The Fragmentary Latin Poets.* Oxford

Curti, E., Dench, E., and Patterson, J.R. (1996) 'The archaeology of central and southern Roman Italy: recent trends and approaches', *JRS* 86: 170–89

DeBrohun, J.B. (1994) 'Redressing elegy's *puella*: Propertius IV and the rhetoric of fashion', *JRS* 84: 41–63

Dégh, L. and Vázsonyi, A. (1976) 'Legend and belief', in D. Ben-Amos (ed.), *Folklore Genres*, 93–124. Austin

Dennett, D.C. (1995) *Darwin's Dangerous Idea: Evolution and the Meanings of Life.* New York

Depew, M. (1993) 'Mimesis and aetiology in Callimachus' Hymns', in M.A. Harder et al. (eds.), 57–77

Desan, S. (1989) 'Crowds, community and ritual in the work of E.P. Thompson and Natalie Davis', in L. Hunt (ed.), 47–71

De Visser, M.W. (1903) *Die Nicht Menschengestaltigen Götter der Griechen.* Leiden

Dorcey, P.F. (1992) *The Cult of Silvanus: A Study in Roman Folk Religion.* Leiden

DuQuesnay, I.M.LeM. (1995) 'Horace, *Odes* 4.5: *Pro Reditu Imperatoris Caesaris Divi Filii Augusti*', in S.J. Harrison (ed.), *Homage to Horace: A Bimillenary Celebration*, 128–87. Oxford

Dumézil, G. (1970) *Archaic Roman Religion*, tr. P. Krapp. Chicago

Edmunds, L. (1990) (ed.) *Approaches to Greek Myth.* Baltimore

Edwards, C. (1996) *Writing Rome: Textual Approaches to the City.* Cambridge

Edwards, M.J. (1991) 'The theology of Catullus 68b', *A&A* 37: 68–81

Elder, J.P. (1962) 'Tibullus: *tersus atque elegans*', in J.P. Sullivan (ed.), *Critical Essays on Roman Literature: Elegy and Lyric*, 65–105. London

Elsner, J. (1995) *Art and the Roman Viewer: The Transformation of Art from the Pagan World to Christianity.* Cambridge

Fantham, E. (1983) 'Sexual comedy in Ovid's *Fasti*: Sources and motivations', *HSCPh* 87: 185–216

(1989) 'The growth of literature and criticism at Rome', in G.A. Kennedy (ed.), *The Cambridge History of Literary Criticism: Volume I: Classical Criticism*, 220–44. Cambridge

(forthcoming) *Ovid: Fasti Book IV.* Cambridge

Faraone, C.A. (1992) *Talismans and Trojan Horses: Guardian Statues in Ancient Greek Myth and Ritual.* Oxford

Fears, J.R. (1981) 'The cult of Virtues and Roman imperial ideology', *ANRW* 2.17.2: 827–948

Feeney, D.C. (1991) *The Gods in Epic: Poets and Critics of the Classical Tradition.* Oxford

(1992) '"Shall I compare thee . . . ?" Catullus 68b and the limits of analogy', in T. Woodman and J. Powell (eds.), *Author and Audience in Latin Literature*, 33–44. Cambridge

(1993a) 'Epilogue: Towards an account of the ancient world's concepts of fictive belief', in C. Gill and T.P. Wiseman (eds.), 230–44

(1993b) 'Horace and the Greek lyric poets', in N. Rudd (ed.), 41–63

(1995) 'Criticism ancient and modern', in D. Innes, H. Hine, and C. Pelling (eds.), *Ethics and Rhetoric: Classical Essays for Donald Russell on his Seventy-Fifth Birthday*, 301–12. Oxford

Fishwick, D. (1987–92) *The Imperial Cult in the Latin West: Studies in the Ruler Cult of the Western Provinces of the Roman Empire*. Leiden

Forbes Irving, P.M.C. (1990) *Metamorphosis in Greek Myths*. Oxford

Foucault, M. (1978) *The History of Sexuality. Volume 1: An Introduction*, trans. R. Hurley. Harmondsworth

Fox, M. (1996) *Roman Historical Myths: The Regal Period in Augustan Literature*. Oxford

Fraenkel, E. (1957) *Horace*. Oxford

　(1960) *Elementi Plautini in Plauto*. Florence

Freccero, J. (1975) 'The fig tree and the laurel: Petrarch's poetics', *Diacritics* 5: 34–40

Fuller, C.J. (1992) *The Camphor Flame: Popular Hinduism and Society in India*. Princeton

Gabba, E. (1991) *Dionysius and* The History of Archaic Rome. Berkeley and Los Angeles

Gagé, J. (1955) *Apollon romain*. Paris

Gale, M. (1994) *Myth and Poetry in Lucretius*. Cambridge

Galinsky, K. (1992) (ed.) *The Interpretation of Roman Poetry: Empiricism or Hermeneutics?*. Frankfurt am Main

　(1996) *Augustan Culture: An Interpretive Introduction*. Princeton

Garnsey, P. and Saller, R. (1987) *The Roman Empire: Economy, Society and Culture*. Berkeley and Los Angeles

Gatz, B. (1967) *Weltalter, goldene Zeit und sinnverwandte Vorstellungen*. Hildesheim

Geertz, C. (1994) 'Life on the edge', *New York Review of Books*, 7 April: 3–4

Gill, C. (1996) *Personality in Greek Epic, Tragedy, and Philosophy: The Self in Dialogue*. Oxford

Gill, C. and Wiseman, T.P. (1993) (eds.) *Lies and Fiction in the Ancient World*. Exeter

Goar, R.J. (1972) *Cicero and the State Religion*. Amsterdam

Goldberg, S.M. (1995) *Epic in Republican Rome*. Oxford

Goodman, M. (1994) *Mission and Conversion: Proselytizing in the Religious History of the Roman Empire*. Oxford

Gordon, R. (1979) 'The real and the imaginary: production and religion in the Greco-Roman world', *Art History* 2: 5–34

　(1990) 'The Roman Empire', in M. Beard and J. North (eds.), 177–255

Gould, J. (1985) 'On making sense of Greek religion', in P.E. Easterling and J.V. Muir (eds.), *Greek Religion and Society*, 1–33. Cambridge

Gouldner, A. (1973) *For Sociology: Renewal and Critique in Sociology Today*. London

Graf, F. (1988) 'Ovide, les *Métamorphoses* et la véracité du mythe', in C. Calame (ed.), *Métamorphoses du mythe en Grèce antique*, 57–70. Geneva

　(1992) 'Römische Aitia und ihre Riten: Das Beispiel von Saturnalia und Parilia', *MH* 49: 13–25

　(1993a) (ed.) *Mythos in mythenloser Gesellschaft: Das Paradigma Roms*. Stuttgart and Leipzig

　(1993b) *Greek Mythology: An Introduction*, trans. T. Marier. Baltimore and London

Grant, M. (1971) *Roman Myths*. London

Greenblatt, S. (1980) *Renaissance Self-Fashioning: From More to Shakespeare*. Chicago

(1991) *Marvelous Possessions: The Wonder of the New World*. Oxford

Griffin, J. (1980) *Homer on Life and Death*. Oxford

(1984) 'Augustus and the poets: "Caesar qui cogere posset"', in F. Millar and E. Segal (eds.), 189–218

(1985) *Latin Poets and Roman Life*. London

Gruen, E.S. (1990) *Studies in Greek Culture and Roman Policy*. Leiden

(1992) *Culture and National Identity in Republican Rome*. Ithaca

Habinek, T.N. (1990) 'Sacrifice, society and Vergil's ox-born bees', in M. Griffith and D.J. Mastronarde (eds.), *Cabinet of the Muses*, 209–23. Atlanta

(1992) 'Grecian wonders and Roman woe: the Romantic rejection of Rome and its consequences for the study of Roman literature', in K. Galinsky (ed.), 227–42

Hall, E. (1989) *Inventing the Barbarian: Greek Self-Definition through Tragedy*. Oxford

(1992) 'When is a myth not a myth? Bernal's "Ancient Model"', *Arethusa* 25: 181–201

Hall, J.M. (1995) 'How Argive was the "Argive" Heraion? The political and cultic geography of the Argive plain, 900–400 B.C.', *AJA* 99: 577–613

Hamerton-Kelly, R.G. (1987) (ed.) *Violent Origins: Walter Burkert, René Girard, and Jonathan Z. Smith on Ritual Killing and Cultural Formation*. Stanford

Hamilton, R. (1992) *Choes and Anthesteria: Athenian Iconography and Ritual*. Michigan

Harder, M.A., Regtuit, R.F., and Wakker, G.C. (1993) (eds.) *Hellenistica Groningana I: Callimachus*. Groningen

Hardie, P. (1986) *Virgil's Aeneid: Cosmos and Imperium*. Oxford

(1991) 'The Janus episode in Ovid's *Fasti*', *MD* 26: 47–64

(1993a) *The Epic Successors of Virgil: A Study in the Dynamics of a Tradition*. Cambridge

(1993b) '*Vt pictura poesis*? Horace and the visual arts', in N. Rudd (ed.), 120–39

Harmon, D.P. (1986) 'Religion in the Latin elegists', *ANRW* 2.16.3: 1909–73

Harries, B. (1989) 'Causation and the authority of the poet in Ovid's *Fasti*', *CQ* 38: 164–85

Harvey, A.E. (1955) 'The classification of Greek lyric poetry', *CQ* 49: 157–75

Henderson, J. (1995) 'Horace *Odes* 3.22, and the life of meaning', *Ramus* 24: 103–51

Henrichs, A. (1987) 'Three approaches to Greek mythography', in J. Bremmer (ed.), 242–77

(1993), 'Gods in action: The poetics of divine performance in the *Hymns* of Callimachus', in M.A. Harder et al. (eds.), 127–47

Henry, J. (1873–92) *Aeneidea*. London and Berlin

Herington, J. (1985) *Poetry into Drama: Early Tragedy and the Greek Poetic Tradition*. Berkeley and Los Angeles

Hickson, F.V. (1993) *Roman Prayer Language: Livy and the Aeneid of Vergil*. Stuttgart

Hinds, S. (1998) *Allusion and Intertext: Dynamics of Appropriation in Roman Poetry*. Cambridge

Hocart, A.M. (1987) *Imagination and Proof: Selected Essays of A.M. Hocart*, ed. R. Needham. Tucson

Hölscher, T. (1993) 'Mythen als Exempel der Geschichte', in F. Graf (1993a) (ed.), 67–87

Hopkins, K. (1991) 'From violence to blessing: symbols and rituals in ancient Rome', in A. Molho, K. Raaflaub and J. Emlen (eds.), *City States in Classical Antiquity and Medieval Italy*, 479–98. Ann Arbor

Horsfall, N. (1982) 'Varro', in E.J. Kenney and W.V. Clausen (eds.), *The Cambridge History of Classical Literature. II: Latin Literature*, 286–90. Cambridge

(1991) *Virgilio: l'epopea in alambicco*. Naples

(1993) 'Mythological invention and poetica licentia', in F. Graf (1993a) (ed.), 131–41

(1994) 'The prehistory of Latin poetry: some problems of method', *RFIC* 122: 50–75

Hunt, L. (1989) (ed.) *The New Cultural History*. Berkeley and Los Angeles

Hunter, R. (1992) 'Writing the god: Form and meaning in Callimachus, *Hymn to Athena*', *MD* 29: 9–34

(1993) *The* Argonautica *of Apollonius: Literary Studies*. Cambridge

Hutchinson, G.O. (1993) *Latin Literature from Seneca to Juvenal: A Critical Study*. Oxford

Iser, W. (1978) *The Act of Reading: A Theory of Aesthetic Response*. Baltimore and London

Jocelyn, H.D. (1966) 'The Roman nobility and the religion of the republican state', *JRH* 4: 89–104

(1967) (ed.) *The Tragedies of Ennius*. Cambridge

(1972) 'The poems of Quintus Ennius', *ANRW* 1.2: 987–1026

(1973) 'Greek poetry in Cicero's prose writing', *YCS* 23: 61–111

Kennedy, D.F. (1993) *The Arts of Love. Five Studies in the Discourse of Roman Love Elegy*. Cambridge

Kenney, E.J. (1977) *Lucretius*. Greece and Rome New Surveys in the Classics 11. Oxford

King, R.J. (1994) *Spatial Form and the Literary Representation of Time in Ovid's* Fasti. Diss. Indiana

Kirk, G.S. (1990) *The Iliad: A Commentary. Volume II: books 5–8*. Cambridge

Knox, P.E. (1986) *Ovid's* Metamorphoses *and the Traditions of Augustan Poetry*. Cambridge

(1990) 'In pursuit of Daphne', *TAPhA* 120: 183–202

Kramer, L.S. (1989) 'Literature, criticism, and historical imagination: the literary challenge of Hayden White and Dominick LaCapra', in L. Hunt (ed.), 97–128

Kuttner, A.L. (1995) *Dynasty and Empire in the Age of Augustus: The Case of the Boscoreale Cups*. Berkeley and Los Angeles

Lamberton, R. (1986) *Homer the Theologian: Neoplatonist Allegorical Reading and the Growth of the Epic Tradition*. Berkeley and Los Angeles

Lane Fox, R. (1986) *Pagans and Christians*. Harmondsworth

Latte, K. (1960) *Römische Religionsgeschichte*. Munich

Lawson, E.T. and McCauley, R.N. (1990) *Rethinking Religion: Connecting Cognition and Culture*. Cambridge

Lee, G. (1974) 'Otium cum indignitate: Tibullus 1.1', in T. Woodman and D. West (eds.), Quality and Pleasure in Latin Poetry, 94–114. Cambridge

Levene, D.S. (1993) Religion in Livy. Leiden

Lieberg, G. (1973) 'Die Theologia tripertita in Forschung und Bezeugung', ANRW 1.4: 63–115

Liebeschuetz, J.H.W.G. (1979) Continuity and Change in Roman Religion. Oxford

(1995) review of Levene (1993), JRS 85: 314–15

Linderski, J. (1982) 'Cicero and Roman divination', PP 37: 12–38

(1986) 'The augural law', ANRW 2.16.3: 2146–312

Long, C.R. (1987) The Twelve Gods of Greece and Rome. Leiden

Mack, D. (1937) Senatsreden und Volksreden bei Cicero. Kiel

MacMullen, R. (1981) Paganism in the Roman Empire. New Haven

Malcolm, N. (1994) Wittgenstein: A Religious Point of View?, ed. P. Winch. Ithaca

March, J.R. (1987) The Creative Poet: Studies on the Treatment of Myth in Greek Poetry. London

Martin, R.H. and Woodman, A.J. (1989) Tacitus: Annals Book IV. Cambridge

Martindale, C. (1993a) Redeeming the Text: Latin Poetry and the Hermeneutics of Reception. Cambridge

(1993b) 'Descent into hell: Reading ambiguity, or Virgil and the critics', PVS 21: 111–50

McDermott, E.A. (1981) 'Greek and Roman elements in Horace's lyric program', ANRW 2.31.3: 1640–72

McKeown, J.C. (1989) Ovid: Amores: Volume II: A Commentary on Book One. Leeds

Méheust, B. (1990) 'Les Occidentaux du XXᵉ siècle ont-ils cru à leurs mythes?', Communications 52: 337–56

Mikalson, J.D. (1983) Athenian Popular Religion. Chapel Hill and London

(1991) Honor Thy Gods: Popular Religion in Greek Tragedy. Chapel Hill and London

Millar, F. (1984) 'State and subject: the impact of monarchy', in F. Millar and E. Segal (eds.), 37–60

Millar, F. and Segal E. (1984) (eds.), Caesar Augustus: Seven Aspects. Oxford

Miller, J.F. (1991) Ovid's Elegiac Festivals. Frankfurt

(1992) 'Introduction: Research on Ovid's Fasti', Arethusa 25: 1–31

Momigliano, A. (1975) Alien Wisdom: The Limits of Hellenization. Cambridge

(1987) On Pagans, Jews, and Christians. Middletown

(1989) 'The origins of Rome', in CAH VII,vol.2, 2nd edn, 52–112

Mommsen, T. (1905) 'Die Akten zu dem Säkulargedicht des Horaz', in Reden und Aufsätze, 351–9. Berlin

Morgan, K.A. (1993) 'Pindar the professional and the rhetoric of the ΚΩΜΟΣ', CPh 88: 1–15

Morris, S.P. (1992) Daidalos and the Origins of Greek Art. Princeton

Myers, K.S. (1994) Ovid's Causes: Cosmogony and Aetiology in the Metamorphoses. Ann Arbor

Nagy, G. (1979) The Best of the Achaeans: Concepts of the Hero in Archaic Greek Poetry. Baltimore

Needham, R. (1972) *Belief, Language and Experience*. Oxford
Newlands, C. (1992) 'Ovid's narrator in the *Fasti*', *Arethusa* 25: 33–54
    (1995) *Playing With Time: Ovid and the Fasti*. Ithaca, NY
Nilsson, M.P. (1920) 'Saeculares Ludi', *RE* 2R.1A.2: 1696–1720
Nisbet, R.G.M. (1961) *Cicero: In L. Calpurnium Pisonem Oratio*. Oxford
Nisbet, R.G.M. and Hubbard, M. (1970) *A Commentary on Horace: Odes I*. Oxford
Nock, A.D. (1972) *Essays on Religion and the Ancient World*, ed. Z. Stewart. Oxford
Norden, E. (1913) *Agnostos Theos: Untersuchungen zur Formgeschichte religiöser
    Rede*. Leipzig
    (1939) *Aus altrömischen Priesterbüchern*. Lund
North, J. (1976) 'Conservatism and change in Roman religion', *PBSR* 44: 1–12
    (1986) 'Religion and politics, from Republic to Principate', *JRS* 76: 251–8
    (1989) 'Religion in republican Rome', *CAH* VII. vol. 2, 2nd edn, 573–624
    (1990) 'Diviners and divination at Rome', in M. Beard and J. North (eds.), 49–71
    (1995), 'Religion and rusticity', in T. Cornell and K. Lomas (eds.), *Urban Society in
    Roman Italy*, 135–50. New York
Ogilvie, R.M. (1981) *The Romans and their Gods*. London
O'Hara, J.J. (1987) '*Somnia ficta* in Lucretius and Lucilius', *CQ* 81: 517–19
Orr, D.G. (1978) 'Roman domestic religion: the evidence of the household shrines',
    ANRW 2.16.2: 1557–91
Osborne, R. (1993) 'Women and sacrifice in classical Greece', *CQ* 43: 392–405
Page, D. (1955) *Sappho and Alcaeus: An Introduction to the Study of Ancient Lesbian
    Poetry*. Oxford
Parke, H.W. (1977) *Festivals of the Athenians*. London
Parker, H.C. (1993) '*Romani numen soli*: Faunus in Ovid's *Fasti*', *TAPhA* 123:
    199–217
Parker, R. (1983) *Miasma: Pollution and Purification in Early Greek Religion*. Oxford
    (1987) 'Myths of early Athens', in J. Bremmer (ed.), 187–214
    (1991) 'The *Hymn to Demeter* and the *Homeric Hymns*', *G&R* 38: 1–17
Parsons, P. (1993) 'Identities in diversity', in A.W. Bulloch et al. (eds.), 152–70
Pease, A.S. (1955–8) *M. Tulli Ciceronis De Natura Deorum*. Cambridge, Mass.
Pettazzoni, R. (1972) 'On common religious impulses', in W.H. Capps (ed.), *Ways of
    Understanding Religion*, 28–32. New York
Pfeiffer, R. (1968) *History of Classical Scholarship from the Beginnings to the End of the
    Hellenistic Age*. Oxford
Phillips, C.R. (1986) 'The sociology of religious knowledge in the Roman Empire to
    A.D. 284', *ANRW* 2.16.3: 2677–773
    (1991a) 'Misconceptualizing classical mythology', in M.A. Flower and M. Toher
    (eds.), *Georgica: Classical Studies in Honour of George Cawkwell*, 143–51. Lon-
    don
    (1991b) '*Nullum crimen sine lege*: Socioreligious sanctions on magic', in C.A.
    Faraone and D. Obbink (eds.), *Magika Hiera: Ancient Greek Magic and Religion*,
    260–76. Oxford
    (1992) 'Roman religion and literary studies of Ovid's *Fasti*', *Arethusa* 25: 55–80
Pighi, G.B. (1965) *De Ludis Saecularibus P.R. Quiritium*, 2nd edn. Amsterdam

Pollini, J. (1990) 'Man or god: Divine assimilation and imitation in the late Republic and early Principate', in K.A. Raaflaub and M. Toher (eds.), *Between Republic and Empire: Interpretations of Augustus and his Principate*, 334–63. Berkeley and Los Angeles

Potter, D. (1994) *Prophets and Emperors: Human and Divine Authority from Augustus to Theodosius*. Cambridge, Mass.

Powell, B.B. (1997) 'From picture to myth, from myth to picture: prolegomena to the invention of mythic representation in Greek art', in S. Langdon (ed.), *New Light on a Dark Age: Exploring the Culture of Geometric Greece*, 154–93. St Louis

Pratt, L.H. (1993) *Lying and Poetry from Homer to Pindar: Falsehood and Deception in Archaic Greek Poetics*. Michigan

Pratt, M.L. (1992) *Imperial Eyes: Travel Writing and Transculturation*. London

Price, S.R.F. (1984) *Rituals and Power: The Roman Imperial Cult in Asia Minor*. Cambridge

   (1987) 'From noble funerals to divine cult: the consecration of Roman emperors', in D. Cannadine and S. Price (eds.), *Rituals of Royalty: Power and Ceremonial in Traditional Societies*, 56–105. Cambridge

Pritchett, W.K. (1976) *The Greek State at War. Part III: Religion*. Berkeley and Los Angeles

Putnam, M.C.J. (1986) *Artifices of Eternity: Horace's Fourth Book of Odes*. Ithaca and London

Rawson, E. (1985) *Intellectual Life in the Late Roman Republic*. Baltimore

Reader, I. (1991) *Religion in Contemporary Japan*. Honolulu

Richardson, N.J. (1993) *The Iliad: A Commentary. Volume VI: books 21–24*. Cambridge

Roberts, M. (1989) 'The use of myth in late Latin epithalamia from Statius to Venantius', *TAPhA* 119: 321–48

Rohde, G. (1936) *Die Kultsatzungen der römischen Pontifices*. Berlin

Roscher, W.H. (1884–1937) *Ausführliches Lexikon der griechischen und römischen Mythologie*. Leipzig

Rose, H.J. (1924) *The Roman Questions of Plutarch*. Oxford

Ross, D.O. (1986) 'Tibullus and the country', *Atti del convegno internazionale di studi su Albio Tibullo*, 251–65. Rome

Rouse, J. (1994) 'Power/Knowledge', in G. Gutting (ed.), *The Cambridge Companion to Foucault*, 92–114. Cambridge

Rudd, N. (1993) (ed.) *Horace 2000: A Celebration. Essays for the Bimillennium*. Bristol

Rüpke, J. (1994) 'Ovids Kalenderkommentar: zur Gattung der libri fastorum', *A&A* 40: 125–36

   (1995) *Kalendar und Öffentlichkeit: Die Geschichte der Repräsentation und religiösen Qualifikation von Zeit in Rom*. Berlin & New York

Scheid, J. (1985) *Religion et piété à Rome*. Paris

   (1987) 'Polytheism impossible; or, the empty gods: reasons behind a void in the history of Roman religion', *History and Anthropology* 3: 303–25

   (1990) *Romulus et ses Frères: Le collège des frères arvales, modèle du culte public dans la Rome des empereurs*. Rome

(1992) 'Myth, cult and reality in Ovid's *Fasti*', *PCPhS* 38: 118–31

(1993) 'Cultes, mythes et politique au début de l'Empire', in F. Graf (1993a) (ed.), 109–27

(1994) 'Les archives de la piété. Réflexions sur les livres sacerdotaux', in *La mémoire perdue. A la recherche des archives oubliées, publiques et privées, de la Rome antique*, 173–85. Paris

Schmidt, E.A. (1991) *Ovids poetische Menschenwelt: Die Metamorphosen als Metapher und Symphonie*. Heidelberg

Schofield, M. (1986) 'Cicero for and against divination', *JRS* 76: 47–65

Schütz, M. (1990) 'Zur Sonnenuhr des Augustus auf dem Marsfeld', *Gymnasium* 97: 432–57

Scullard, H.H. (1981) *Festivals and Ceremonies of the Roman Republic*. London

Seaford, R. (1994) *Reciprocity and Ritual: Homer and Tragedy in the Developing City-State*. Oxford

Selden D.L. (1992) '*Ceveat lector*: Catullus and the rhetoric of performance', in D.L. Selden and R. Hexter (eds.), *Innovations of Antiquity*, 461–512. New York and London

Skutsch, O. (1985) *The* Annals *of Quintus Ennius*. Oxford

Slater, N.W. (1993) 'Improvisation in Plautus', in G. Vogt-Spira (ed.), *Beiträge zur mündlichen Kultur der Römer*, 113–24. Tübingen

Smith, J.Z. (1978) *Map is Not Territory: Studies in the History of Religions*. Leiden

(1982) *Imagining Religion: From Babylon to Jamestown*. Chicago and London

(1987) 'The domestication of sacrifice', in R.G. Hamerton-Kelly (ed.), 191–235

Smith, K.F. (1913) (ed.) *The Elegies of Albius Tibullus*. New York

Solodow, J.B. (1988) *The World of Ovid's* Metamorphoses. Chapel Hill.

Sourvinou-Inwood, C. (1991) *'Reading' Greek Culture: Texts and Images, Rituals and Myths*. Oxford

Sperber, D. (1975) *Rethinking Symbolism*, tr. A.L. Morton. Cambridge

(1985) *On Anthropological Knowledge. Three Essays*. Cambridge

Staal, F. (1989) *Rules Without Meaning: Ritual, Mantras and the Human Sciences*. New York and Bern

Taussig, M. (1993) *Mimesis and Alterity: A Particular History of the Senses*. New York and London

Timpanaro, S. (1988) *Cicerone: Della divinazione*. Milan

Tomlin, E.W.F. (1974) *The Last Country: My Years in Japan*. London

Toynbee, J.M.C. (1947) 'Ruler-apotheosis in ancient Rome', *NC* ser.6, 7: 126–49

Tresp, A. (1914) *Die Fragmente der griechischen Kultschriftsteller*. Giessen

Turcan, R. (1988) *Religion romaine. I: Les Dieux. II: Le Culte*. Leiden

Usener, H. (1896) *Götternamen: Versuch einer Lehre von der religiösen Begriffsbildung*. Bonn

Van Straten, F. (1993) 'Images of gods and men in a changing society: Self-identity in Hellenistic religion', in A.W. Bulloch et al. (eds.), 248–64

Vasaly, A. (1993) *Representations: Images of the World in Ciceronian Oratory*. Berkeley and Los Angeles

Vernant, J.P. (1983) *Myth and Thought Among the Greeks*. London

Versnel, H.S. (1987) 'What did ancient man see when he saw a god? Some reflections on Graeco-Roman epiphany', in D. van der Plas (ed.), *Effigies Dei*, 42–55. Leiden

(1990) *Inconsistencies in Greek and Roman Religion 1. Ter Unus. Isis, Dionysos, Hermes: Three Studies in Henotheism*. Leiden

(1993) *Inconsistencies in Greek and Roman Religion 2. Transition and Reversal in Myth and Ritual*. Leiden

Veyne, P. (1988) *Did the Greeks Believe in their Myths? An Essay on the Constitutive Imagination*, trans. P. Wissing. Chicago

Vian, F. (1952) *La Guerre des géants: le mythe avant l'époque hellénistique*. Paris

Waghorne, J.P. and Cutler, N. (1985) (eds.) *Gods of Flesh/Gods of Stone: The Embodiment of Divinity in India*. Chambersbury, PA

Wallace-Hadrill, A. (1982) 'The Golden Age and sin in Augustan ideology', *P&P* 95: 19–36

(1988) 'Greek knowledge, Roman power', *CPh* 83: 224–33

(1993) *Augustan Rome*. Bristol

(1994) *Houses and Society in Pompeii and Herculaneum*. Princeton

Warde-Fowler, W.W. (1911) *The Religious Experience of the Roman People*. London

Wardman, A.E. (1976) *Rome's Debt to Greece*. London

(1982) *Religion and Statecraft among the Romans*. London

Weinstock, S. (1957) 'Victor and Invictus', *HThR* 50: 211–47

(1971) *Divus Julius*. Oxford

West, D. (1995) *Horace Odes 1: Carpe Diem*. Oxford

West, M.L. (1978) (ed.) *Hesiod: Works and Days*. Oxford

(1988) 'The rise of the Greek epic', *JHS* 108: 151–72

Wheeler, K.M. (1993) *Romanticism, Pragmatism and Deconstruction*. Oxford

White, R. (1991) *The Middle Ground: Indians, Empires, and Republics in the Great Lakes Region, 1650–1815*. Cambridge

Whitehead, N. (1995) 'The historical anthropology of text: the interpretation of Ralegh's *Discoverie of Guiana*', *Current Anthropology* 36: 53–74

Whitman, J. (1987) *Allegory: The Dynamics of an Ancient and Medieval Technique*. Oxford

Williams, G. (1968) *Tradition and Originality in Roman Poetry*. Oxford

Wills, J. (1990) 'Callimachean models for Ovid's "Apollo-Daphne"', *MD* 24: 143–56

Wiseman, T.P. (1974) 'Literary genealogies in late-Republican Rome', *G&R* 21: 153–64

(1985) *Catullus and his World: A Reappraisal*. Cambridge

(1989) 'Roman legend and oral tradition', *JRS* 79: 129–37

(1995) *Remus: A Roman Myth*. Cambridge

Wissowa, G. (1912) *Religion und Kultus der Römer²*. Munich

Woodbury, L. (1985) 'Ibycus and Polycrates', *Phoenix* 39: 193–220

Woolf, G. (1994) 'Becoming Roman, staying Greek: Culture, identity and the civilizing process in the Roman East', *PCPhS* 40: 116–43

Yunis, H. (1993) review of Mikalson (1991), *CR* 43: 70–2

Zanker, P. (1988) *The Power of Images in the Age of Augustus*, trans. A. Shapiro. Ann Arbor

Zetzel, J.E.G. (1992) 'Roman Romanticism and other fables', in K. Galinsky (ed.), 41–57

Zipes, J. (1987) *The Complete Fairy Tales of the Brothers Grimm*. New York and London

General index

Index of passages discussed